RELATIONSHIP
STYLES & PATTERNS

Relationship
Styles & Patterns

Kenneth Garett, Ph.D.

and

William Rose, Ph.D.

Williams Publishing
Books that Inform, Educate and Inspire

RELATIONSHIP STYLES & PATTERNS
By Kenneth Garett Ph.D. and William Rose, Ph.D.

Publisher's Note
This publication is designed to provide accurate and authoritative information in regard to the subject matter covered. It is sold with the understanding that the publisher is not engaged in rendering psychological, financial, legal or other professional services. If expert assistance or counseling is needed, the services of a competent professional should be sought.

For information contact: Williams Publishing, 4766 Park Granada Suite #209, Calabasas, California 91302, Telephone: (877) WP-Books.

Cover Design by Wild Beast Productions.
Text Design by Arte Moderno.

Distributed in U.S.A. by BookWorld Companies

Library of Congress Catalog Card Number: 98-88423
ISBN 0-9666906-9-9

Publisher's Cataloging-in-Publication
(Provided by Quality Books, Inc.)

Garett, Kenneth.
    Relationship styles & patterns / Kenneth Garett and
    William Rose. -- 1st ed.
    p. cm.
    Includes bibliographical references.
    LCCN: 98-88423
    ISBN: 0-9666906-9-9

    1. Man-woman relationships. 2. Interpersonal
    relations. I. Rose, William, 1954- II. Title. III.
    Title: Relationship styles and patterns

    HQ801.G37 1999   158.2
                          QBI98-1473

We dedicate this book to our families and friends.
May your lives be blessed as ours is being touched by your
love and kindness.

Acknowledgments

We wish to acknowledge the invaluable efforts and support of the following people who helped make this book possible. Kerry Rose, whose tremendous commitment of time and effort in providing editorial direction was so very helpful and appreciated. Sheryl Rose, whose technical assistance and skills made such a great difference. Kenneth Rose, whose ongoing support made this project possible. Marilyn Perlin, Lou Perlin and Tamara Garett for their never-ending encouragement, love and guidance, for which we are so fortunate to have. We also gratefully acknowledge the inspiration provided by Dr. Marvin Meyers.

CONTENTS

CHAPTER 1

ABOUT RELATIONSHIPS

Have you ever wondered how some people achieve satisfying relationships and others just can't? Is there some reason why relationships work well in some areas of your life but not in others? Have you ever thought about why some people who remain single are perfectly happy while others are crazed when unattached? All people go through some transitions in their lives that are marked by periods of stress and isolation. But do you know people who always complain about not meeting the right person? Is there a pattern to any of this? Yes. And the more you know about your particular pattern, how you create or prevent intimacy in your life, the more you will be able to cultivate and sustain happy, healthy relationships of your choice.

We believe that people have different Relationship Styles, their own unique ways of being in the world. These "styles" are the reason why some are capable of sustaining intimate relationships and why some remain alone. Our academic and professional clinical experience have led us to this viewpoint. There is no mystery about finding Mr. or Ms. Right, or a satisfying relationship! In exploring the ways men and women relate to each other, we will examine the ability to establish intimacy and the ability to sustain it. To sustain an intimate relationship involves many things. Because you are not the same person as your partner, it is important to learn how to work through issues by understanding your individual Relationship Styles. **People who are honest with themselves, who desire to share with others and who are available, will find many opportunities to include others in their lives. In the final analysis, it is these qualities (honesty, desire and availability) that will allow us to enjoy successful and lasting relationships.**

This book provides the tools for you to make an accurate character analysis and helps you to identify your personal Relationship Style. **Importantly, we will show you how your style affects your relationships with others.** Not only do we illustrate your patterns, we provide ways to enhance the ones that work and modify the ones that don't.

We all know that life isn't fair and often circumstances are not under our control. Sometimes our response to negative experiences (loss, divorce or betrayal) is to close off our emotions and ideas. This may lead to a cycle of isolation, fear and difficulty in making new commitments. All we ask is that you bring the desire to be happy, healthy and honest in your relationships and we will bring some exciting new tools.

We cannot promise to change you completely. For instance, if you are basically shy and introverted, we cannot turn you into someone who is extroverted and outgoing. Or, if you are an extrovert by nature, we cannot make you into someone more reserved. **We can provide you with the information to help you modify some of your behaviors so**

that they do not interfere with your potential to have successful and satisfying relationships.

Relationship Stages

The first stage of a relationship is the fantasy stage. All is magic and love. This stage typically lasts from several weeks to several months (and even years for those who are very lucky). When the initial excitement of finding a once-in-a-lifetime love wears off, a new picture emerges and many relationships begin to have problems. "The honeymoon is over." Arguments may occur as a result of seeing that your partner is not perfect after all. **This is when you begin to understand that you and your partner are different.** The ability to maintain the relationship depends on addressing these differences. To sustain the relationship you each have to accommodate, or in effect reconcile "the difference" within yourself. It is during the second phase of a relationship, the reality stage, that we attempt to reconcile these differences. Your ability to sustain the relationship beyond the second stage, in which you and your partner accommodate each other's imperfections and keep going, depends upon love, commitment, communication, openness, and awareness. At this phase, understanding your Relationship Style and that of your partner is critical.

The third phase of a relationship is the accommodation stage. It is essentially the period of learning, practicing, integrating and adapting. Here you create long-term solidarity in the relationship in order to sustain it. Unfortunately most relationships never reach this point. Many people get married during the first stage of their relationship and never reach the accommodation stage. When they have been married for some time they may become surprised at how extremely chaotic their relationship is once the fantasy stage is over. They usually did not spend enough premarital time together to experience the chaos that the relationship could eventually have. It is important, therefore, that before people get married, they spend enough time together in an effort to understand each other's Relationship Styles. This will prepare them for the inevitable loss of illusion that comes when the magic fades. **A better understanding of your relationship style and that of your partner will help with the overall development and strength of your relationship.**

When a relationship's fantasy stage continues for a few years, the participants usually are not confronting the day-to-day issues that may cause conflict. Long-distance relationships and those in which the partners are not truly available (i.e., married, in other relationships, not really interested) illustrate this. In all cases, individuals must understand and examine objectively their Relationship Style and that of their partner. Tools obtained in therapy to learn how to communicate and solve problems in a troubled or shaky relationship are always helpful.

Childhood Histories

The way an individual views and acts on conflict is often rooted in early development. It is common in couples therapy to have the partners share and explore some of their past and current family issues with the other person present.

The impact of this sharing and disclosing is often profound and moving. In counseling, issues related to physical, emotional, or sexual abuse are amplified when shared. **It is important to understand that issues of abuse or deprivation during the childhood years often create conflicts. Because they have not been identified or dealt with, they still affect the current relationship.**

These conflicts may take different forms; however, they tend to share enough similarities that we can now describe or predict patterns in Relationship Styles. This allows us to use the tools of therapy and communications to help a person understand different ways of relating to others. Some people have difficulty sharing their inner thoughts and feelings with others on any but the most superficial levels. It is often harder for these people to benefit from therapy or self-learning techniques. **The key to change is a personal desire to do so.** This desire must be present to increase self-awareness and personal insight.

In the following chapters we hope to help you understand your personal Relationship Style. **Our goal is twofold. First, we want to help improve your ability to understand how you relate to the world, and how those around you relate to you. Second, we want to help you enhance your relationships with others by exploring the particular patterns in your relationships.** As mentioned before, you must have a desire to look honestly at yourself (not a simple challenge for most of us). This is an important step toward improving the overall quality of your relationships.

We will introduce and extensively use the terms Accommodator, Director, and Isolator. **We cannot stress**

enough that these terms have neutral meanings! There are both positive and negative attributes for every Relationship Style. As you read on, whether your style is Accommodator, Director or Isolator, continue to ask yourself, "Is this how I function?" And, if so, "Are there some things about the way I function that are not working for me?" And, maybe most crucial, "What can I do to make some effective changes in my Relationship Style?" We believe that understanding your personal Relationship Style will help you attain success and happiness in your life.

This book is different in many ways from other self-help books. Our book does not focus on the differences between men and women, or inherent communication patterns based on gender. Instead, it goes one step farther in exploring how people live and interact. **Men and woman are human beings and all humans of either sex are as likely to exhibit one of the three Relationship Styles. All three styles cut across cultural bias and economic status. And all three Relationship Styles can affect any aspect of life for better or worse.**

In our more than 35 years of professional experience, we have seen clients with many of the problems that will be discussed in this book. We will do our best to illuminate the nature of relationships, and to provide you with additional tools, skills and philosophies to help you better understand your life.

CHAPTER 2

WHAT IS YOUR RELATIONSHIP STYLE?

We are excited and ready to get you on the path to successful relationships. We have designed a scale to identify and measure your individual Relationship Style. This is not a test with deep hidden meanings. The results will help you understand your own personal style in relating to others. It is also a valuable tool in helping you understand the Relationship Styles of your loved ones.

Please answer the following 21 questions frankly and rapidly. Your first response to an item is usually the most accurate. After you complete the test we will help you score and evaluate the results. Now, go ahead and take the test and please do not look at the scoring page first. We do not want to influence your responses in any way. Remember, there are no right or wrong answers! This is a learning tool. The goal is to improve your awareness and self-understanding, and to have some fun!

RELATIONSHIP ASSESSMENT SCALE

Please circle the score that most applies to you.
Does Not Apply = 1 / Applies Somewhat = 2 / Applies = 3

1. There are usually extended periods of time, more than six months, between my long-term relationships.

    1 / 2 / (3)

2. I tend to start a new romantic relationship almost as soon as I break up with someone.   (1) / 2 / 3

3. In the past, people have accused me of being controlling.

    (1) / 2 / 3

4. I am older than 30 (for females), or 35 (for males), and have never been married.   (1) / 2 / 3

5. I am frightened at the prospect of being alone.

    (1) / 2 / 3

6. I like to make specific vacation plans when I travel with my spouse or significant other.   (1) / 2 / 3

7. I am uncomfortable in large, unstructured social settings, such as restaurants, large parties, or formal affairs.

    (1) / 2 / 3

8. I do not like rocking the boat, so I keep things to myself.

    (1) / (2) / 3

9. When I start dating someone it is hard for me not to try to improve their way of dressing and behaving, which can make them feel criticized.   1 / 2 / 3

10. It is hard to stay in a long-term relationship. I tend to look for new choices when things get sticky and the honeymoon period is over.   1 / 2 / 3

11. Just to please my partner or date, I will go to a movie that I really do not care to see.   1 / 2 / 3

12. I demand a great deal of attention from my partner and feel angry when I am neglected.   1 / 2 / 3

13. I have a set standard on which I rate my current or potential partner.   1 / 2 / 3

14. I will change my habits in order to accommodate my significant other.   1 / 2 / 3

15. I am more comfortable paying the household bills and would be reluctant to give this responsibility to my spouse.   1 / 2 / 3

16. I find it difficult to establish intimate contact with others, and feel that my life is more lonely than I would like.   1 / 2 / 3

17. In reviewing my life, I find I have only lived on my own very briefly or not at all.   1 / 2 / 3

18. I prefer to be the initiator of sexual activities.

1 / 2 / 3

19. I believe falling in love is more difficult for me than for most of my friends.   1 / 2 / 3

20. I am careful not to hurt someone's feelings.

1 / 2 / 3

21. I am comfortable in expressing my own opinions in most social gatherings.   1 / 2 / 3

Scoring Your Results

After you have scored your responses the following guidelines will help you interpret the results. You will notice that we have divided the results into three general categories: Isolator, Accommodator, and Director. Remember, none of these labels is better or worse than the others. Each type has its own unique characteristics; each has both strengths and weaknesses. Remember, this exercise is not to label yourself, but to gain some important self-knowledge.

Scoring Key

Write your score for each of the questions next to the corresponding number below. For example, if your score on question 1 was 3, write 3 next to the number 1 below. If you scored 2 on question 2, then write 2 next to the number 2 below, and so forth until all the items have a numerical score. The next step is to add up each column and write your total score below it:

Isolator Items (I) Accommodator Items (A) Director Items (D)

Isolator Items (I)	Accommodator Items (A)	Director Items (D)
1.	2.	3.
4.	5.	6.
7.	8. 2	9.
10. 3	11. 7	12. 2
13. 2	14. 2	15.
16.	17.	18.
19. 2	20. 2	21.
Total (I):	Total (A):	Total (D):

With your totaled scores, you are now able to find out where your results place you on the scale.

A high score in any of the three Relationship Styles is 17 to 21.

Moderate scores are in the range of 11 to 16.

Low scores are less than 10.

Your Relationship Style code type may be a pure type (I, A, or D), which is indicated by having only one high score or moderate score. Other Relationship Style code types have at least one high (or moderate) score followed by a second lesser (high or moderate) score. The following combinations are possible: IA, ID, AI, AD, DI, DA.

While interpreting the results of your Relationship Assessment, it is important to realize that it is the strength of the trait that will be critical. The highest scores one can achieve on the Relationship Assessment Scale are uniform for all three styles. If your score approaches the maximum (21) in any of the categories, it is safe to assume that you probably share a strong characteristic of that Relationship Style. Importantly, a moderate score may be interpreted as a personal relationship tendency as opposed to your usual style of operation. Try to be fair with yourself. A moderate score may be interpreted as your dominant style if your other scores are also lower. The goal is not to create a negative self-image.

Now that you have scored the Relationship Assessment Scale, let's see what it all means. And importantly, let's find out how you can use this information to improve your life! First we'll describe the different relationship types, along with some of the various issues that face all of us in our relations with others as friend, lover, parent, child, employee, employer, student, teacher, and so on.

CHAPTER 3

THE THREE BASIC RELATIONSHIP STYLES

Isolators

Isolators have an essential tendency, whether they acknowledge it or not, to draw away from others. This condition of pulling away is the result of various psychological tendencies created early in childhood. **Isolators may be very social individuals but they experience major barriers in establishing and maintaining primary relationships.** They frequently live alone throughout much of their adulthood. If you are an Isolator do not despair, you are not truly alone. The phenomenon of social isolation has increased statistically in America since the 1960s. This means that there are now a greater number of single individuals just like you who establish lives that are essentially self-contained.

Psychoanalyst Erik Erikson was a major contributor to our present understanding of the psychological developmental stages in life. He believed that a basic mistrust of others will eventually lead adults to withdraw into themselves, especially when they experience conflict. Erikson described this developmental conflict as "intimacy versus isolation." The primary focus of early adulthood is how we resolve this conflict. The underlying mistrust that characterizes an Isolator's view of others often makes it difficult for him or her to make a long-term commitment.

The negative consequences of isolating are depression, feelings of emptiness, and cynicism. These symptoms are one of the primary reasons people seek psychological and psychiatric services and have stimulated the growth of a multibillion-dollar pharmaceutical industry in the development and sales of antidepressant medications (whose prescribed usage is not limited to Isolators).

Childhood experiences provide the historical basis for an Isolator's mistrust. In addition, Isolators frequently have unhealthy role models for intimacy, which results in the development of their style. An illustration of an unhealthy family model that produces Isolators is that of Mary and her children. Mary has three adult children, none of whom ever married. Each is financially successful and free of any major health problems. They are all long past early adulthood and well established as part of the unmarried population. This is due in large part because Mary, although a sweet and loving mother, was married to an alcoholic who abused her in front of the children. Even with many years of therapy, the essential distrust that evolved from this made up the children's view of marriage and commitment and has not been overcome. Thus Mary's children became Isolators.

If the results of your Relationship Assessment Scale indicate that your primary relationship style is that of an Isolator, this knowledge does not condemn you to a lifetime of loneliness and depression. It is a challenge to you to understand the cause of your current isolation and to take steps to increase the enjoyment of your current relationships. **Whatever the reasons for the basic mistrust that underlies your view of love and commitment, once you acknowledge it the journey to healing begins.** In later chapters we will provide you with activities that help you challenge and empower yourself to overcome the limitations created by isolating.

Directors

Directors have an essential tendency to exaggerate their sense of power and control. When the Director fears helplessness he or she seeks to dominate situations to avoid this feeling. Intimate relationships often create or mimic a feeling of helplessness. If your Relationship Assessment Scale results indicate that you are a Director, you probably do not like feeling dependent and vulnerable. Often Directors are the children of parents who were bossy, domineering and dictatorial toward them. Birth order has traditionally affected the acquisition of this interpersonal style. Many Directors are the oldest or the only child.

The initial response to the term "Director" can be a negative one, but there are many positive aspects of possessing a strong and domineering personality. Directors frequently are driven toward leadership roles. Many express themselves in politics. Therefore, if their style is tempered by awareness and humility, they can be great contributors to the common good. And in a positive light, Directors are willing to take risks and can inspire others if they have charismatic qualities.

On the downside, Directors are prone to be dogmatic, which can inspire a wide range of reactions among those who interact with them. We will describe these interactions using a variety of psychological theories, including transactional analysis, Gestalt, and systems work. At the most positive end, with insight, Directors can become enlightened leaders and assertive, effective members of society. On the negative end, Directors can be damaging to others and ultimately self-destructive.

Self-awareness is essential to the success of a Director in establishing positive relationships and meaningful life experiences.

Accommodators

Accommodators are individuals who seek the company of others and dislike isolation. Accommodators tend to marry young and to remarry quickly if they divorce. They get along well with others and tend to join and conform well in large organizations. Their primary desire is to be included. In this way they experience a sense of competency. When isolated through divorce or other life circumstances, Accommodators feel depressed, confused, and overwhelmed. On the positive side Accommodators are supportive, cooperative and affiliating. On the negative side they are passive, needy and clingy. The unique manner in which these individuals cope with their need for affiliation determines whether they become more supportive than dependent.

There is a natural tendency for Accommodators and

Directors to connect. Their need systems are mutually compatible. Accommodators dislike isolation and are drawn to individuals who manifest power and control. This attraction may be an unconscious or a poorly understood attempt to balance or complete themselves psychologically. If someone fears competition and lacks assertiveness, then it is an easy solution to select a mate who has those qualities. Unfortunately, sometimes this leads to enormous hostility and if left unresolved, it may erupt and destroy the relationship. **The major challenge that Accommodators face in forming healthy unions is based on how they can control their fear of isolation.** The use of the term "codependency" as an explanation for unhealthy relationships refers to an extension of Accommodators' "selling out" their integrity to avoid isolation. In later chapters we will illustrate this more clearly with case studies from therapy.

CHAPTER 4

UNDERSTANDING YOUR RELATIONSHIP STYLE

As we have stated, one of the greatest human challenges is the development of self-understanding and self-awareness. The ability to understand of how we interact and build relationships forms the basis of most of the literature pertaining to interpersonal psychology, marital therapy, and social psychology. Karen Horney, a well-respected psychologist, proposed that there are primarily three ways in which humans interact: They either go toward, stay away from, or are against others. In other words we bond with, avoid, or antagonize others.

These positions also relate to the results of your Relationship Assessment Scale. Isolators tend to stay away from others and find a sense of security and control through distancing themselves. Accommodators move toward others, seeking communion in relationships and organizational groups. Directors seek leadership roles or situations where they can dictate the terms of their interactions with the world.

No one is completely one type. We are a complex interaction of different needs. For example, Isolators may eventually marry, even if the process of commitment is not easy. Doubt and fear may still underlie their decision-making process. If the high score of your profile was that of an Isolator, let's look at some of the implications.

Isolators - A Deeper Look

In general, Isolators tend to have difficulties adjusting to social situations. In high school, they often resist joining the crowd. Frequently, they are highly creative, artistic individuals who are inspired by their "inner" world. If your score on the Isolator questions were four or more points higher than your scores on either the Accommodator or Director questions, your tendency is to isolate. More balanced scores, where your Isolator scale is only slightly higher than your Accommodator scale, indicate a balance between your need for privacy and for social interaction. This balance may in fact be a healthy interaction, which leads to establishing a good long-term relationship, especially with someone who is more of an Accommodator.

In returning to our inventory, you will note that Isolators often admit having difficulty establishing and maintaining long-term relationships. They usually marry later in life, if at all, and are sometimes prone to developing depression. If your Relationship Style is to isolate, the first step is to admit that you do Isolate yourself. It is neither bad luck nor chance that led you to this position. In Chapter 6 we will present some exercises that will help Isolators overcome their personal limitations and develop a more effective interpersonal lifestyle. The key is to identify and accept your level of isolation.

We have stated that Isolators were affected profoundly by childhood experiences. Culture and genetics also have an impact on the development of one's Relationship Style. Many social scientists and biogenetics experts believe these predispositions are inherited and that Isolators are basic introverts. This is what has been described as the "nature versus nurture argument"; our genes versus our environment. In addition to this, cultural factors also play an important role. For example in many Asian societies, isolation is culturally reinforced.

Developmental factors interwoven with early childhood experiences affect the growth of personality, character, and Relationship Style. Isolators are nurtured in environments lacking intimacy. Divorce, family neglect, and emotional abuse lead a child to withdraw into him or herself for protection. We see this often in individuals raised without constant parental interaction, like children placed in boarding schools or other institutional settings.

Where interaction between biogenetic factors and the environment creates the dynamics for withdrawal, the same family situation can generate individuals with different Relationship Styles. Isolators often grow up in families with siblings who are Accommodators or Directors. The precise reason why siblings are so different cannot be completely explained by birth order, genes or environment alone. It is one of the mysteries that underlie the uniqueness of human character.

The Mix: Isolator-Accommodators, Isolator-Directors

Isolators can also have the characteristics of either Accommodator or Director as indicated by their scores on the Relationship Assessment Scale. Isolators whose Accommodator score is only slightly lower than their Isolator score have a balance between their need for privacy and need for contact with others. They may pick or choose when they affiliate or not. Isolators with secondary high characteristics of Director may have more difficulty in personal relationships and are more fearful of the loss of control that accompanies commitment. They may resist counseling and develop lifestyles based on their own unique parameters. Due to underlying distrust, an Isolator may feel that romantic love and inti- mate contact come at too high a price. A lack of participation creates much of the sadness and hopelessness that accom- pany the lives of Isolators. In coming chapters we will offer an action plan for Isolators to confront their style of living and empower them to increase their social contacts.

Accommodators - The Need for Balance

Because we live in a society where social interaction is considered good, accommodating other people is a highly re- inforced social style. Even the basic concept of our demo- cratic system has equated social responsibility with social participation. Unfortunately, there is a thin line between be- ing socially active and socially dependent. This line often marks the difference between a healthy, involved individual and one who may be "needy" or what is often called "codependent." Look carefully at your Relationship Assessment Scale results. If your score on the Accommodator scale is higher than 15 and this score is more than four points higher than your results on either the Director or Isolator scales, then you probably have a strong need for accommodation. This neediness makes you likely to be vulnerable to the following situations. Read and think about the following four statements and we will explore your situation in greater detail.

1. I am living or have lived with someone who I feel is not right for me. This is partially out of fear of being alone.

2. I am working in a job that I really do not like because the prospects of changing employment are scary.

3. I seldom discuss unfilled sexual desires with my partner for fear that I will hurt their feelings.

4. I do things for other people even when I don't want to.

It is important to be honest with yourself because if two or more of these statements applied to you, your need for accommodation has taken a self-destructive turn. You are probably afraid of asserting yourself and are now more likely intent on pleasing others than fulfilling your own needs. "Codependency" is a term coined from popular psychology. It describes people whose needs to affiliate are so compelling that they give up personal control and independence. This is a very unhealthy situation and often leads to great dissatisfaction and unhappiness. In Chapter 5 we will explore a case that illustrates this situation.

The Mix: Accommodator-Director, Accommodator-Isolator

A balance of accommodation tendencies is the key to a healthy social life. **Balance is also the key to enhancing and strengthening long-term committed relationships.** A score of 14 or lower on your Relationship Assessment Scale indicates your need for accommodation is in the midrange. This midrange score, if coupled with a Director score within four points, describes someone who has a healthy balance between a desire to relate well to others, while maintaining a positive ability to be assertive. Accommodators constantly balance the need for dependence and independence. A classic scenario is that of a woman who is married to an alcoholic. This is a woman whose accommodation needs are unhealthy. Her fear of being alone outweighs a rational ability to leave. Her need to accommodate binds her to someone who is destructive to himself and those around him. Unfortunately, this happens all too frequently. A rational approach would suggest that the person should not remain in a relationship with someone who is on the road to destruction. The twelve-step program Co-dependents Anonymous is a place where unbalanced Accommodators can seek help in coping with problems related to having partners who are both controlling and self-destructive.

Directors - Learn to Moderate Your Power

Directors are top dogs. They dislike it when people tell them what to do. They are often resented by others and (ironically) sometimes simultaneously revered. This situation lends itself well to Eric Berne's theories of transactional analysis. In transactional analysis, Berne created a way to help us understand the mechanisms by which we operate and relate to one another. From a transactional viewpoint, most Directors have overdeveloped "parents." "Parents" are the part of the personality that influences us to do things. We hear or remember a parent saying "you should" and "you must." When individuals have overactive "parents," they often have an inability to respect others' boundaries and desires. We actually develop these overactive transactional "parents" from our own real parents. The process becomes integrated in our personalities. The clinical term to describe this is "introjection." In a sense we "introject" our experiences with our parents. The behaviors they modeled for us become ingrained in the ways we respond to the events around us. The old adage "like father, like son" reflects this process well.

A Relationship Assessment Scale score higher than 16 on Director indicates an individual's strong desire to dominate his or her place in the world. The delicate balance between being a bully and being a leader is often a matter of self-development, inner awareness, and understanding.

Many of the greatest contributions to modern societies have been made by Directors who have relegated their energy and leadership skills toward the common good. Directors who avoid self-confrontation and psychotherapeutic treatment may see either as a weakness. The most potentially dangerous Relationship Style is that of an angry, unfulfilled Director.

Psychoanalyst and theorist Alfred Adler examined the development of feelings of inferiority and its compensation in individuals. Adler believed that during childhood most individuals experience feelings of inadequacy. These feelings of inadequacy may be related to simply being "smaller" or as complex as having learning difficulties. Negative or critical parenting may push the feelings of inferiority to a greater level. Children respond to this assault in diverse ways. They can either develop low self-esteem, becoming an Isolator or Accommodator, or overcompensate with feelings of superiority and arrogance. When a child overcompensates with feelings of superiority he or she often becomes domineering, aggressive, and at times antisocial. In other words, an angry, poorly nurtured self creates a "bully." A "bully" is most often a Director lacking both social consciousness and compassion. The leadership style of some of history's (and let's not forget current) political dictators demonstrate the "Director" style in its most detrimental form.

The Mix: Director-Accommodator, Director-Isolator

In contrast, something very positive happens when a Director can balance the difference between a need for power and a desire to aid the common good. Directors can achieve remarkable things if their trait is tempered with humility and compassion toward others.

Directors tend to seek out Accommodators during the course of their lives. This can lead to a healthy balance of differences in most cases. In worst-case scenarios it becomes a form of master and slave type of relationship and can prove very damaging to both parties. Two Directors can live together. They will, however, tend to argue and struggle over turf issues. If the level of control isn't too severe, the couple can share a dynamic and challenging relationship in which each party challenges the other's sense of security and forces growth.

Directors whose Accommodator score are close to, but lower than their Director score may show a healthy respect for others with leadership ability. The key concern for those readers with high Director scores is to identify their tendencies and work on moderating their need for power by developing concern for others. We present exercises to help Directors with this in Chapter 6.

CHAPTER 5

COMPARING YOUR RELATIONSHIP STYLE WITH OTHERS

This chapter presents examples of both balanced and unbalanced individuals in each of our three categories. You may want to look for your style and score and compare them to our examples. Remember, the cases here are examples and while they may be similar to your own, they are not you. **They do, however, illustrate the important aspects of how the Relationship Assessment Scale differentiates and describes behavior.**

Unbalanced Accommodator
38-Year-Old Female
Relationship Assessment Scale:
Accommodator 19, Isolator 12, Director 7

Michelle has been married for the past three years. Michelle lived with her parents until they died, spending the last six years before her marriage with her father. Michelle was very dependent throughout her life. She was born prematurely and suffered from health-related problems as an infant and toddler. When she entered kindergarten, she was found to be a slow learner and placed in special education classes. Her parents never totally grasped the nature of Michelle's problems. Their other children all were self-directed and left home after high school. Two of her siblings graduated from the state university.

Michelle's school-related difficulties were compounded by her timidity and feelings of insecurity. She rarely dated and was a virgin until her late twenties. Michelle's style was to please others; her greatest desire was to fit in. When frustrated or angry, she tends to feel overwhelmed and often suffers migraine headaches.

Michelle had difficulty finding employment. She attempted to work in a preschool as an aide, but was unable to complete the community college class work to receive a preschool teaching credential. She has continued working in preschools, but has had long periods of unemployment during the summers and when personnel changes were made.

Michelle married a neighbor who had been married before and who worked for the gas company as a meter reader. His relationship assessment depicted him as a Director with a secondary trait of an Accommodator. He is comfortable with Michelle's compliant attitude and tends to criticize her poor housekeeping skills and forgetfulness. Michelle's husband drinks excessively on occasion, but doesn't consider himself an alcoholic, although two years ago he was arrested for drunk driving. Michelle's fear of being alone makes her unable to contemplate confronting her husband's drinking. He handles financial issues in the home and is only minimally bothered by his wife's limited earning capacity. Michelle was referred for psychotherapy by her internist when he noted that her chronic headaches had no medical basis.

Follow-up: Michelle is learning to assert herself and state what she needs. Her headaches, related to her conflicted emotions, are improving as she learns in therapy to speak up when her husband's behavior is inappropriate. Michelle continues to express fear when discussing her problems in therapy. However, she is developing and improving her self-esteem and is now more assertive in expressing herself and her needs regarding family matters. She has developed the strength to confront her husband's abusive behavior. Her husband is responding in a positive way by decreasing his abusive manner with her and seeking help for his problems with alcohol.

Balanced Accommodator
42-Year-Old Female
Relationship Assessment Scale:
Accommodator 14, Director 12, Isolator 9

Kendra, a regional sales representative, is married and has a nine-year-old daughter. Kendra's husband is a landscape contractor. He showed a balanced profile with Accommodator and Isolator equally weighted at 12. Kendra's parents were hard-working people who had four children; Kendra was the third child. She seldom had problems in school and joined a number of social organizations both in high school and church.

Kendra attended community college, later transferred to a state university, and completed a B.A. in marketing. She dated and had two long relationships, the second of which led to her marriage. Kendra was a volleyball player in high school but has gained weight since the birth of her daughter and has had difficulty getting back to her pre-pregnancy weight.

In her job as a sales representative, she shows a good team attitude and has had two promotions. Kendra is described as a levelheaded and pleasant team leader. She balances her need to affiliate with others with a healthy ability to direct her life and set appropriate limits with her peers.

Admissions of an Accommodator

The following dialogue comes from an interview with a man who has a typical Accommodator Relationship Style. Alan is 48 years old and divorced. He is a contractor by trade and has a 28-year-old daughter and a two-year-old granddaughter:

"I had a great childhood. I had supportive parents and grandparents who motivated me. As a teenager, I had a lot of friends. I was a hippie, I even went to Woodstock. I really miss those times. Everything was much more simple then. . . .

"I recently lost my father after a long illness. Being an only child made it difficult for me. It would have been nice to have had someone to share the grieving process with. My mother passed away several years ago. She was an alcoholic, although you would never have known it. My family definitely had its secrets. . . .

"My marriage lasted seven years. It ended because I got tired of her accusing me of running around, which I didn't do.

I am currently single again after being in another relationship with a woman for 18 years. She was very controlling and we became incompatible. I find it really hard to function in a controlled-type situation. My career has been fine and I have enjoyed success. It is in relationships that I have had my share of problems. If anything, I trust too much, especially when I first meet someone. Then if things don't feel right I start to pull back the trust. I tend to take people at face value. I am a people person. I can handle social situations, and I prefer to be around people. If I get uptight inwardly, I never let it show on the outside. I meet people wherever I go and it is just easy for me. I tend to fit in well with others and I generally get along with most people . . . I do have problems relating to people who are very controlling. It has taken me a long time to figure this out."

Follow-up: Alan is doing quite well and has reconnected with a long-time girlfriend. They are planning to be married and are in couples counseling together. He is learning about adult children of alcoholics issues and how theses issues affect him many years after experiencing abuse. Like many of his generation, he has learned how his conflicts gave him a distrust of people holding power and authority. In his maturity he has learned to understand his feelings regarding those he sees as trying to exert control over him. He is now more aware of these issues and is more assertive and expressive with those close to him.

Confirmed Isolator
43-Year-Old Male
Relationship Assessment Scale:
Isolator 17, Director 12, Accommodator 8

Gerald was briefly married at age 19 while living in Mexico as a student. This marriage was chaotic. After his numerous adulterous encounters, Gerald left his wife. Then he returned, and they persisted in an unstable pattern of reuniting and breaking up for two and a half years until they were finally divorced. Gerald has not lived with another woman since his divorce. Currently, he resides in Brazil, and spends part of each year in the United States visiting his brother.

In order to understand Gerald's isolation it is useful to review his childhood. Gerald was the second of three boys. His parents divorced when he was three years old and his father moved out of state, not paying child support or seeing Gerald again until he was 19. Gerald's mother, overwhelmed by the divorce and plagued with chronic depression, sent Gerald and his brothers to boarding school and sleep-away camp in the summer.

Gerald was a gifted student and was advanced from second to fourth grade. At age 14 Gerald finally was living at home with his mother. His older brother was at a university out of state. Gerald called his older brother and requested his help in convincing his mother to allow him to live on a kibbutz in Israel, where he remained until he graduated from high school two years later. Admitted to a state university at age 16, he did well in his course work, but dropped out after his sophomore year and returned to his mother's home, where he worked in the post office. Gerald eventually moved to Mexico to study and complete his B.A. in business. It was during this period that Gerald met his wife. Unfortunately, Gerald was not committed to her and left her alone on many evenings while pursuing new liaisons in local clubs. The marriage soon ended.

After his divorce, Gerald worked in sales for a number of companies and because of his extreme frugality was able to save a substantial amount of money. He lived alone in studio apartments until he could quit working at age 29 and could live abroad in various countries. In order not to spend his savings, Gerald's social life consists of pursuing one-night stands at bars. Seldom do his relationships last more than a few months, with frequent long periods between romantic interludes.

Gerald spends much time alone in his room reading books in various languages; he is fluent in French, Spanish, Portuguese and Hebrew. He fantasizes marrying and settling down in a foreign country but has shown no behavior that would convince anyone that he will act on it.

Follow-up: Unfortunately Gerald is completely unwilling to accept any form of therapy. He continues to blame others and external factors for his lack of intimacy. He is completely unwilling to change in any significant way that might improve his relationships with others.

Balanced Isolator
50-Year-Old Male
Relationship Assessment Scale:
Isolator 12, Accommodator 10, Director 8

William lives with his wife, who is nine years his junior. William was married many years before, but his first marriage ended in divorce after four years. William works as a roofing contractor. He enjoys spending his free time land-scaping and improving his home. William and his wife chose not to have children. They have numerous pets to which they are quite devoted.

William was the youngest of two boys. His parents divorced after he was grown and both have since remarried. William grew up appreciating hiking, bird watching, and fishing. He avoids urban environments and crowded parties. William's second marriage seems to be much more compatible than his first. His wife travels regularly for the company she is employed by and they seem genuinely content with each other.

William enjoys spending time on the Internet and reading. He spends much of his free time at home, but is cordial and receptive to neighbors and friends. Generally, William is level-headed and disciplined. He is a person you can rely on.

Insight of an Isolator

The following dialogue is from an interview with Laura. Her results on the Relationship Scale indicate that she has the style of an Isolator. Laura is 35 years old, divorced, and lives with her 9-year-old son. Her interview revealed the following:

"I like to be by myself, and I am comfortable this way. At times, when I do feel nervous, being by myself helps me feel more at ease. If I get lonely, then sometimes I want to be with other people. . . .

"When I was growing up my mother was a screamer, and my father was very quiet or he wasn't around. My

mother was nervous, and she would yell a lot at everything. I realize now that this was just her way. Even as a child, I liked being by myself most of the time. As a teenager when I was upset with things I would just go into my room. In high school I didn't do any extracurricular activities. I did what I was supposed to do, my work, and then I would go home. I didn't realize it then, but now I see that I was very critical of myself. . . .

"In college I didn't date at all until my junior year. I went to some parties but I didn't like them. I just didn't think I was pretty enough; I just didn't feel comfortable. I found friends who also didn't like to go to parties either. I was 22 when I got married, right after I graduated from college. At the time, I didn't know what marriage was. This was the only man I ever dated or got involved with. He was the first person that I ever had sex with. But I was never comfortable with the idea of getting married. I was a extremely nervous and I wasn't eating. I lost a lot of weight. Later on I couldn't believe that I did marry, and then I felt that I should try to make it work. . . .

"I didn't like it when he would come home and just want to have sex right away. He would literally just walk through the door, sit down with me, and just start thinking that I could just jump right into bed. . . . I am basically an insecure person. When it comes to work, I just do things that I know I can do easily, things that I won't have to struggle with. Sometimes I feel that I am selling myself short. I don't have much confidence and I tend to avoid dealing with issues. I would like to accomplish more. . . .

"Eventually I got a divorce. Since then, it is still hard

for me to go out. But I get very lonely and I am aware of it. I don't want to disappoint myself, so I know I have to go out even though I am not comfortable. I don't even know if I want to marry again; even the thought of living with someone is just something I am not comfortable with."

Follow-up: Laura is learning to adjust to a single life. She continues to share her dreams about falling in love and getting married someday. A major hurdle for her is her ability to make herself available to others, especially those who are also single. She continues in a pattern of focusing all her attention on the needs of her young son, while ignoring her own. Sadly, like too many other Isolators, she has accepted that her lot in life is to remain single. In therapy, Laura may learn that to remain single is only one option and not the only option that she has.

Tyrannical Director
37 Year-Old-Male
Relationship Assessment Scale:
Director 18, Accommodator 12, Isolator 8

Michael is a physician. He originally wanted to be an attorney but his parents discouraged that choice. He has been married twice. Both marriages ended in bitter divorces, which have continued with custody battles and ongoing hostility. Michael has two daughters from his first marriage, who live with him. His first wife was accused of cocaine abuse and after many months of court proceedings, Michael was awarded custody of his daughters.

Professionally, Michael was a high achiever. After completing medical school, he became a cardiac surgeon and briefly taught at a medical school. He eventually began working in a hospital and opened a private practice.

Michael's second marriage was shorter and riddled by explosive arguing and conflict. Michael's second wife was a model and an actress. She is a glamorous woman, and when they first met at a party she was drawn to Michael's bravado and flamboyant style. She attempted to become a mother for his daughters after he moved the family to another state, when he accepted a position at a prestigious hospital as the chief cardiac resident. This move made it difficult for the girls' natural mother to see them regularly. His second wife's frustration at his excessive hours at the hospital and their lack of time together led to increased arguing. After the birth of their son they divorced. Michael immediately started dating younger women. He especially likes women who work as models for *Playboy* and similar magazines. Michael drives an expensive sports car and maintains a condo at a resort in Mexico.

Michael is a controversial figure at his hospital. He frequently feels his colleagues are trying to undermine him and is regularly embroiled in conflicts with the hospital administration. Michael loves his children, but is prone to throw temper tantrums and display excessive emotion while in their presence. Financially, he is overextended, but he continues to maintain his expensive tastes. Michael tends to affect people in either extremely positive or extremely negative ways. He definitely leaves an impression one way or another.

Follow-up: Michael just doesn't learn from his past experiences. He was recently successful in a lawsuit with his ex-wife and is now involved with a young woman who is financially dependent upon him. Michael needs and enjoys power and control. The women that he has relationships with tend to submit and oblige him, at least for awhile. Unfortunately, his children have suffered emotionally a great deal from his behavior and messy divorces. After resolving one war, Michael finds a new one. He continues to battle the administrators at his hospital and is still fighting with an ex-business partner. Michael remains a lawyer's dream client, as his legal fees tend to exceed most people's annual incomes.

Director with Insight
29-Year-Old Female
Relationship Assessment Scale:
Director 14, Accommodator 12, Isolator 8

Amy is remarried after a brief first marriage. She is completing a master's degree in clinical social work, having returned to college in her mid-twenties. Amy was the youngest of two children. Her parents divorced when she was five years old and after that contact with her father was rare. He apparently felt little responsibility toward her and moved out of state when Amy was nine years old. Amy's mother then remarried a man with a history of alcoholism who had difficulty handling the responsibilities of two small children. In addition, his relationship with his stepchildren was tainted with jealousy and resentment. Amy witnessed physical antagonism between her brother and her stepfather, which led her brother to leave home abruptly at age 14 to live with an aunt. Amy would stand up to her stepfather's verbal abuse and developed a strong personality, which makes her, at times, assertive and unbending. This led to much quarreling with her first husband, who was the spoiled youngest child of wealthy parents. They met in the Bahamas where Amy was doing a photo shoot in her early twenties. She is a beautiful woman who had a short-lived career as a model prior to pursuing her current career in social work.

Amy, however, has a very soft and endearing character. She is especially talented when it comes to establishing positive relationships with children. Amy's second husband has a son from a previous marriage and they are bonded and loving. She prides herself on being able to be a positive step-parent. There is a balance between Amy's need for control and her desire to affiliate with others. She worries excessively about her weight and minor physical imperfections. She enjoys dancing and has many female companions, some of whom describe her as domineering. Amy has plans for the future and intends to control the outcome of her life. She still has occasional verbal confrontations with her second husband, but they never reach the level or intensity of those during her first marriage.

Follow-up: Amy is an example of a Director striving for balance. Although at times she continues to be bossy and a perfectionist, she wants a healthy relationship and is learning to change the things that don't work. She has become much more affectionate and thoughtful with those around her. Although it is difficult for her, she is learning to accept herself the way she is and her body image has improved in spite of years of worrying about her weight and physical appearance.

Confessions of a Director

The following dialogue comes from an interview with Diane, whose scores on the Relationship Scale placed her in the Director range. Diane is 31 years old, and works as a sales representative for a computer firm. Here are some excerpts from her interview:

"I just don't like limits or certain boundaries set on me. Sometimes I interfere too much with other people and try to get my way. Looking back over my life I have always been this way. My parents divorced when I was two. When my mother remarried it was nice, because my stepfather was great. He was probably one of the nicest men in the world and he loved children. In school I was the type of person who had to be in charge of things. I always had to be the leader of my group. I always had to tell the kids what we would do. I think they appreciated it because otherwise we would have had a boring childhood. . . .

"I was sixteen when I had my first child. Sometimes I wonder where I was at mentally at that time, but I think it was just a way to get out of the house. I was angry with my mother for divorcing my stepfather and I wanted to get away from her. She then dated other men who were just horrible. They were alcoholic and abusive. I was the only one who would tell her what losers her boyfriends were. One of her boyfriends sexually abused my little sister. . . .

"After I became pregnant at sixteen, I had to deal with it. I wasn't upset about it, I just had to decide what I was going to do and move on. I graduated from high school and went on from there. I started making decisions to take control of my life.

The relationship with the father of my first child was not good. We were young, and he was a really jealous person. And his jealousy really bothered me. I thought our relationship was a waste of time and we separated. When I was 20 I got married and had another son. Unfortunately, this relationship didn't last and we got a divorce. I think my relationships today are much improved. I am now planning to marry the father of my oldest son. He has changed a lot and is much more mature now. . . .

"I enjoy my job as a sales representative. I can set my own time and see whom I want to see.

It is nice not having anybody to answer to and just do what I want. I just like everything to be exactly as I want it to be. I just want things done the way they need to be done, or the way I feel it needs to be done. My boyfriend and I get into conflicts because I want to have my own way. I get mad when things aren't done the way they should be. If he does things his way, which in my opinion is not right, I get mad. I just like to get things done my way. This is very important to me.

"It would be nice if I was able to take a deep breath and just relax. But it is difficult for me to do this. Sometimes I just don't know how to stop. I think I have a fear of someone else making decisions for me. It is really difficult for me to trust anyone. I think there are very few people you can trust. I developed this attitude just growing up the way I did. Obviously, if you can't trust your mother, who can you trust? I still get angry with her. I have tried to forgive her, but when I think about our experience, I get upset. I told her what I think about her, and how lousy it was. . . .

"I do regret having put my children through the divorce,

because divorce is so hard on everyone. I just think of what could have been, or what I would have done differently. Sometimes I wonder where my life would be. Overall, I feel that I have control of my life now. I am also very satisfied with who I am and how I feel. In terms of my life, I think I have geared it to where I want it to be."

Follow-up: Diane's personality was greatly affected by the abuse she experienced as a child. She doesn't allow people to get close to her and she appears more comfortable this way. She works at presenting the outward appearance of stability and happiness, while internally she is conflicted by emotional turmoil. Diane refuses to allow herself any sexual release and substitutes fantasy for pleasure and control for intimacy. This need for control prevents Diane from experiencing intimacy within a relationship and prevents her from ever really loving anyone other than her children. Diane is beginning to address these issues in her therapy. Although has been difficult for her to accept that other people may have valid opinions, she is learning that she needs to make some changes in her life. By understanding her Relationship Style, Diane has started the process of increasing her self-awareness and improving her relationships with others.

CHAPTER 6

HOW TO IMPROVE YOUR RELATIONSHIPS

For years we have told clients the following dumb joke: How many psychologists does it take to change a light bulb? One, but the light bulb really has to want to change. We all have lifestyles for which we must take responsibility in order to change. Understanding the past, our parents, or our childhood is essential. Altering a pattern is never easy. Modification is only possible if we are motivated to attempt it.

By now, you have identified your relationship style and its basic characteristics. Any style, Accommodator, Director, or Isolator, carries with it both positive and negative aspects. Our goal is to keep the good and throw out the bad, destructive or unhealthy behaviors that keep us from satisfying relationships and from being happy with ourselves as we are. When you allow yourself to change those things that prevent you from relating better with others the results are beneficial not only to you but to your loved ones.

Let's take a personal inventory and examine ourselves even closer. First we will explore different aspects of each relationship style and then offer a rehabilitation plan to bring balance to your life.

The Isolator

Let's list three negative and three positive consequences of being an Isolator.

Negatives:

* I don't like being alone and if I keep on this way I will be alone in later years.

* I get depressed periodically, especially when I am not dating anyone.

* The process of dating has become annoying and an endless cycle of disappointment.

Positives:

* I am not vulnerable to being hurt by anyone.

* I don't trust my ability to stay in long-term relationships; therefore, I don't test that ability.

* I abhor long-term relationships and seek variety.

Your childhood:

* What example of love and commitment did your parents model for you?

* How much positive reinforcement, in terms of love and support, did you receive as a child?

* Did you leave childhood with a basic distrust of love and commitment?

Your adolescence and adulthood:

* How did you view yourself at 13 years old? Did you feel that you had a peer group or were you isolated?

* Did you fit in at school and participate in organizations and on teams?

* Did you find the early steps in dating difficult? Did you delay dating or participate sporadically until your

late teens?

* Did you have trouble falling in love? Were you deeply disappointed by your early love experiences?

* If previously married, do you feel that divorce has made you more cynical or wounded about your ability to make a new commitment?

Please answer these questions in detail. Write down your answers. Review them often. They are a reminder of the key elements that have created your current isolation.

How does an individual become an Isolator? Let's explore the reasons why you became an Isolator. Understanding the process gives you the choice to change or modify your behavior.

An example of an Isolator's history might be:

My childhood was marred by poor role models of love and commitment. My parents divorced, and never really completely forgave each other for the divorce. I can't recall seeing them act affectionately toward each other. My stepfather was cold and rejecting. I never felt he really accepted me; he only tolerated me.

My adolescence was difficult. I suffered from acne and was late maturing physically. I had difficulty dating and did not have a committed relationship until I was close to 20. This relationship ended when my girlfriend said she wanted her freedom and broke up with me after 18 months of living together. I became severely depressed, and it took over a year to regain any sense of myself.

My underlying belief is that relationships do not last, and if they do, I am probably not the type who is able to sustain one. I seldom confront this underlying belief, and actually never completely confronted it until today. I blindly keep seeking one encounter after another with women until I retreat back into myself, frustrated and discouraged.

Basically, the underlying psychological makeup of an Isolator is that of a discouraged child. Isolators never witnessed love as a child, and therefore continue to think it doesn't exist. It is this "discouraged child" that is now in control of their destiny.

THE DISCOURAGED CHILD GROWS UP

Steps Towards Modifying Your Isolating Behavior-The Plan:

Sometimes the results are small or take time. Things will change if you want them to and if you take action.

Step One: Acknowledgment: My Role in the Problem

* I acknowledge that I am an Isolator. My way of behaving is my primary reason I am alone.

* I need to look at my insecurities regarding my ability to have a loving relationship.

* I am ready to confront these beliefs every day, and to initiate creative activity to challenge them.

Step Two: Acknowledging My Role in Changing

* I have the choice today to increase my social contacts.

* What I have been in the past is irrelevant to my choice today.

* Instead of isolating today I will do the following: (Fill in your activity)

<u>This activity will demand that I participate and interact with people</u>.

* I am as capable as anyone else of having a loving relationship. I am tired of convincing myself that I am different from people in committed relationships.

* List other activities you will do this week to increase your social contacts.

* No excuses will be accepted.

* Review and revise this plan in writing from week to week. Sunday evening is an ideal time to write a new plan.

<u>Example of a Plan</u>:

* I will rehearse and memorize several positive self-statements that will challenge my childhood belief systems. Using positive self-statements is a very effective therapeutic tool.

For example:

* I haven't always been alone in the past, and the future is up to me.

* I am as capable as anyone else of experiencing love.

* Many people who fall in love years later are still with the same person.

* I am capable of handling change. The boat that I am in isn't so terrific anyway; it is time that I rock it a little.

Many people find using a counselor or therapist works especially well for the purpose of clarifying goals and creating a plan for change. Find a mental health professional who has a track record of being productive, willing to challenge you, and capable of assisting you in helping create effective changes. It is important when choosing a therapist to find one who understands the principles of self-confrontation, but is also supportive, encouraging, and open to discussing ways of moving forward, one who helps you learn to challenge yourself in developing a positive self-image. Joining a well-run therapy group is also a very positive way of confronting your isolation on a weekly basis.

The Accommodator

Now let's list three negative and positive consequences of being an Accommodator.

Negatives:

* I am frequently treated poorly, but I am afraid to stand up against that treatment.

* I experience anxiety regularly, especially when I am unsure of how to respond to ambiguous situations.

* I feel unable to make any plans or choose any independent activities.

Positives:

* I don't like being alone, and as an Accommodator, I don't have to face it.

* It is hard to handle transition. Even if my current relationship is defective, I am used to it and can cope with it.

* I usually agree with the decisions of others and do not experience as many conflicts as other people tend to.

Your childhood:

* Did you experience fear of being alone as a child?

How did your parents respond to this apprehension?

* Did the idea of living on your own frighten you, and did you ever attempt it in spite of this fear?

* Did you find the time you spent alone as a teenager uncomfortable, and attempt to find activities to prevent time alone?

Your adolescence and adulthood:

* Were you resistant to the idea of going away from home overnight with school programs or sleep-away camp?

* Did you tolerate bad treatment from school friends and fear confronting them?

* Did you feel uncomfortable in leadership or public speaking situations?

* Once you began dating, did you feel vulnerable that your boyfriend's last girlfriend would cause you to break up?

* Did you attempt to accommodate your friends' needs in order to preserve the relationship?

Please answer these questions completely. Write out your answers and review them weekly. These questions will remind you of the origins of your accommodative style. Remember, knowledge is empowering, but knowledge alone does not produce change.

A summary of an Accommodator's history may appear as follows:

I was the youngest of three children and was pampered as the baby of the family. My oldest sister was eleven years older than me, and she treated me like her daughter. I had few responsibilities until I started high school. My homework was done for me by my sister whenever I couldn't figure it out. The first time I attempted to sleep over at a girlfriend's house my mother came to pick me up early because I was crying and frightened.

I was a good, compliant student, and seldom got in trouble in elementary school. I never sought leadership roles but would go along with the crowd. Once my friends started dating, I was less secure around boys than I thought they were. I was excited when one of the boys on the football team took an interest in me and asked me out. I wasn't really ready to have sex with him, but he was very persistent and we did after about six dates. We didn't use contraception. I got pregnant approximately two months later. When I told him, he became angry and started becoming more distant and unavailable. I decided to have an abortion at my parents' insistence, even though I felt it was morally wrong. Following the abortion, I became extremely anxious, and had my first panic attack. I was taken to the ER and given Valium. They explained that I wasn't having a heart attack but was frightened. I continued to have panic attacks and was referred for psychotherapy by my family physician.

What this might mean now:

You are still that insecure, needy child who was overprotected. You developed a poor sense of self by pleasing others. How will you help this dependent girl develop a sense of identity and autonomy?

THE INSECURE, NEEDY CHILD LEARNS TO STAND UP FOR HERSELF

Steps to Change Accommodating Behavior-The Plan:

<u>Step One</u>: Acknowledge my role in the problem.

Be aware that you are a people pleaser, and that your dependent, unassertive behavior has been developed over your life.

* I acknowledge that I am an Accommodator and one who will please people rather than follow my own convictions.

* I must realize that underlying my people pleasing is the basic belief that I need others to like me, and am willing to mold myself around their needs, not my own.

* I am willing to confront this belief daily, until I begin to acknowledge certain illogical and self-destructive aspects of my belief system.

<u>Step Two</u>: Acknowledge my role in changing.

List three behaviors that illustrate your tendency to please others: (Here are some examples)

* I agree to do things I don't want to do.

* I stay on the phone even when I want to hang up so as not to offend anyone.

* I agree to have sex with my boyfriend when I do not want to so he won't be upset with me.

To break the pattern:

* I will work on breaking my old patterns by not accepting the three just mentioned behaviors.

* I will remind myself every day that, "I do not need

anyone's approval to approve of myself." This will be my motto! It is a simple step in assertiveness training, but one I really need.

* I will consider joining an assertiveness training group, group therapy or a co-dependents anonymous group where my focus will be to work on my negative behavior. If I do not feel ready to join a group at this point, I will consider psychotherapy with a therapist who understands my motivation and will help encourage me .

* I need to accurately review my history of pleasing others and denying my own feelings. I will write down alternatives to the way I behave and I will review these alternatives with a trusted friend and accept their feedback. If I am in therapy, I will review them with my therapist. I will slowly try to implement one of the alternatives.

<u>An example</u>: I tend to go along with whatever my husband wants to do on our evenings out, even if I would really prefer to do something else.

<u>Alternatives</u>: The next time we go out, I will suggest an activity, and tell him I would appreciate him trying my idea this time. I will learn to use "I" messages that make direct statements without blaming, as a way of expressing my desire for a chosen activity. For example: "I would like to go to the new foreign film, which sounds interesting. I would like you to come, too." This is a clear, positive, direct, noncritical request. It is definitely not the manner in which Accommodators usually ask for things.

The Director

Let's list three negative and positive consequences of being the Director.

Negatives:

* I push people away and have had people reject me because of my behavior.

* In many ways, I maintain a barrier to intimacy and experience moments of being totally isolated.

* Power is a two-edged sword. Power gives me control. But I also feel stressed and frustrated with myself and others, and research indicates I am physically and emotionally straining my health.

Positives:

* I tend to get what I want.

* I feel powerful and in control when I act in a controlling manner.

* People perceive me as strong, invulnerable, and independent.

Your childhood:

* Who was the domineering, controlling individual in your childhood?

* How did that person make you feel when giving you directions?

* Do you think, without being aware of it, you may have adopted some aspects of that person's behavior style?

Your adolescence and adulthood:

* Were you frequently one of the leaders of your peer group?

* Did you feel angry when your ideas were not readily accepted?

* Have you been accused of being pushy, bossy, and domineering?

* In intimate relations, do people get angry at you? Have you been accused of being a poor listener?

Directors are often the most resistant to see how their relationship style affects others. They are concerned with getting their way. This limits their ability to commit to change. Directors may do well by admitting that they are Directors, rather than prematurely agreeing to a modification program.

A brief summary of the Director's history:

I was the oldest child in my family. I had two younger siblings, and I always felt in charge of them. My parents gave me the responsibility to look after them on the playground. I tended to put down my brother and sister verbally and pick on them physically. My father owned a business. He worked hard and came home tired and cranky. He tended to bark orders at us: "Clean your room, get ready for school, go to bed." He was a good person, but always seemed to be in a hurry and tended to be impatient and irritable. If we didn't do as we were told we would get a spanking.

In school, I would speak out in class and enjoy being noticed. In the neighborhood, I organized sports and games and was considered a leader. I would try to act cool as a way of showing my power. Although normally nervous around girls, I would push myself to talk to them. Eventually I achieved some sense of comfort and security with the opposite sex.

My underlying belief is that it is better to control your life, or others will control you. It is dog eat dog out there, and no one will take care of you but yourself. Dad always said that the meek will not inherit the earth, and I guess I developed his basic philosophical attitudes. He always told us life wasn't a popularity contest and that I should do what I want, disregarding what others thought of me.

Your underlying psychological structure as a Director is the need to control. As a child you were treated insensitively and have adopted that style of getting your needs met. Underneath there may be a sad and disappointed person. For many Directors, this sadness only appears when they are abandoned by the person they have controlled for many years.

THE SAD AND INSENSITIVE CHILD BECOMES HEALTHY AND HAPPY

Steps to Modify Behavior for Directors-The Plan:

It is important to remember that Directors are consistently resistant to change, so be patient with yourself.

Step One: Acknowledgment of my role in the problem.

* I acknowledge I am a Director and that my need to control is the primary reason I have had problems with others.

* I need to confront my beliefs about success and my ability to have more sharing relationships with others.

* I will observe my behavior and begin to challenge it on a daily basis.

Step Two: Acknowledgment of my role in changing.

* When I use the words *should, must, always,* and

never, I am probably being controlling. These are parental words and tend to put people off.

* I will practice increasing my use of the word "I."
* I will stop trying to bully people that I care for.
* I will ask the significant others in my life for feedback on whether my approach is becoming less dogmatic and more democratic.

Most Directors do not seek therapy or accept change unless something happens that reveals a very painful consequence of their behavior. An example is marital discord, as when the Director is rejected by a spouse who is fed up with being dominated and humiliated. In order to save the relationship, the Director is forced into therapy, at least temporarily.

Directors who are aware of the effect of their behavior on others and who humanize themselves are healthier and happier. Their efforts and skills are valuable. The difference between a tyrant and a leader is that a tyrant uses his power for himself and a leader uses his power for the good of others. Communications training can have a significant impact in helping a Director to develop a more insightful and caring way of relating to the world around him.

CHAPTER 7

RELATIONSHIP STYLES INTERACTING

The goal of this chapter is to show you how your Relationship Style works when you interact with others. We do not live in a vacuum. We constantly relate to other people. Your environment is affected by your unique Relationship Style and your interactions with others. For example, a Director will affect others in a decidedly different manner, in terms of interacting, than an Isolator.

Eric Berne, in his book *Games People Play*, developed transactional analysis, a system to help simplify and systematize our ways of interacting. Berne wrote that each person has three basic sub-personalities or ego states: a parent who likes to give orders and directions, an adult who is reasonable and democratic, and a child who is selfish, playful, and at times resentful. For example, your parent component will make comments such as, "You should clean your room," or "Why don't you listen to me?" Your adult will negotiate what can be done to settle problems, by saying, for example, "Do you want me to help you?" or "I am interested in you." Your child is the playful and spontaneous part of you. It might say, "Let's call in sick from work today," "I'm resentful when no one listens to me," "Let's make love," or "Leave me alone."

These three subpersonalities exist in each of us. They

compete, so to speak. And these sub-personalities behave differently in creating our unique Relationship Style. For years psychologists have studied people's interaction patterns, and can identify which subpersonality, child, parent or adult state is present in an individual at any moment. Then it is easy to translate any interaction between two people into a "transactional" study of the three states or subpersonalities. There are benefits of using Berne's transactional analysis to help us understand our three Relationship Styles (Accommodator, Director and Isolator). We can then more effectively look at the way we relate to others in terms of our Relationship Styles.

For example, two people who are married and who are both Directors will tend to parent each other. This might mean trying to criticize each other and to control each other's decision-making process. When this is the case, it almost always leads to power struggles and arguing. Once the couple understands that they are both Directors, and arguing is an unavoidable aspect of being in a relationship with another strong-willed individual, they can begin to develop skills that let them argue and solve conflicts more democratically (or at least more effectively with less harm to their relationship). Directors may typically interact in the following way:

He: Honey, you should start studying. Your exams are in three weeks.

She: I did study last night.

He: But you will have to study every day; these are major exams.

She: Stop nagging me.

He: **(Unhealthy response)** No matter what I say, you take it the wrong way.

(Healthy response) I didn't mean to nag, I am just concerned. I know how important passing these exams is to you.

In this interaction summary, being parental and giving advice leads to a defensive and angry child response. Once a pattern is established, the results can be angry, hurt feelings, or a heightened sense of mutual respect. The final conclusion of any transaction pattern depends on our awareness of how we communicate, and most importantly, the effect it has on others.

Different character styles tend to communicate in very different manners. A few basic themes:

Isolators tend to keep quiet when criticized. This leads them to harbor resentment, much like a child who feels bullied by his or her parents and can't fight back on equal terms. An example of a typical Isolator interaction pattern may be:

He: I am leaving~ next month to study abroad.

She: When will you be back?

He: In six months.

She: Don't you love me?

He: I planned this before we started dating; you knew that.

She: I knew, but we weren't serious then.

He: **(Unexpressed)** I hate it when women try to get me to commit myself when I am not ready. **(Expressed)** I will see you when I come back.

This summary hints at the disintegration of a relationship. He is afraid of making any type of emotional commitment. His hidden, frightened child prevents him from responding directly to her desire for assurance and support. What he

takes away from the interaction is a feeling of being pres-
sured, and she, a sense of being abandoned. These are the
precursors for the relationship's demise. She is an
Accommodator needing support, reassurance, and closeness.
He is in denial of his strong tendencies toward isolation and
is sabotaging another chance at intimacy. Patterns and transactions of this sort create the themes of our emotional life.

A typical Accommodator transactional pattern might
be:

She: I sent you a card yesterday. I hope you received it.
He: No, I haven't received it yet.
She: I was thinking about you, and it seemed to be the
perfect card.
He: That was very thoughtful of you.
She: **(Unexpressed)** I really hope you like me and will
ask me out again. **(Expressed)** Well, I just wanted to
say hello.

This dialogue demonstrates her hesitant style and
subtle attempt to acquire emotional feedback. She is seeking
support, looking for some affirmation that he is emotionally
bonding with her. To be direct with him is too threatening, so
she chooses a more indirect manner of expressing this need,
and in so doing reaffirms the Relationship Style of an
Accommodator. Whether this relationship has any possibil-
ity of lasting will depend on whether he is willing to embrace
her needs. If he has a strong need for control or affiliation as
well, this may happen. It does not, however, guarantee a
healthy relationship, just one that might continue. **Establishing healthier, productive relationships comes from
knowing your Relationship Style and embracing the man-**

ner in which you relate that style to others. To do this involves understanding the principles of transactions in your Relationship Style and applying them to your behavior.

In review: Directors tend to be controlling and bossy. When unchecked, this leads to arguing, compliant responses, or resentment from spouses, friends and others. Directors need to be open to feedback. Directors need to realize that it is acceptable and probably preferable to ask others such questions as, "Did I upset you? Did you feel criticized?" A Director who seeks feedback in this manner will become more effective in creating healthy relationships and will be seen by others as less controlling.

Accommodators need to realize that it is acceptable to ask for what you want more directly. This involves the risk of being disappointed and accepting that you will not always get what you want.

Isolators should understand that the manner in which they use their thoughts or ideas to avoid direct emotional confrontation is a result of their fear of closeness. Isolators must also learn to risk being direct to overcome their fear of intimacy. In the next chapter, we will explore in greater detail how each Relationship Style expresses emotions.

CHAPTER 8

YOUR EMOTIONS AND RELATIONSHIP STYLE

There are basic differences in the manner in which each Relationship Style reacts to the world. We all express ourselves through a mix of rhythms of behavior and emotions. Emotions are essential aspects of being human. The diversity of our emotional range is what makes us different from other species. Infants demonstrate a range of emotions from birth; when hungry, tired, or frustrated, they cry. They exhibit anger to discharge physical tension. In moments of contentment, infants appear happy. At approximately eight to nine months of age, most babies develop a fear reaction or aversion to strangers. This distrust of strangers reveals itself by physical rejection of nonparental figures when these people attempt to hold or come too close to the baby. Fortunately, this fear/aversion response diminishes once the toddler has had repeated positive contacts with new individuals.

These basic responses create a simplified manner of analyzing emotional contact. The infant demonstrates anger or frustration when its needs are not met, or when physically uncomfortable. It feels happiness or contentment when fed, sleeping, or stimulated in a pleasing manner. Later in the first year of life, a fear or distrust response develops in reaction to strangers. In neutral situations, infants and children demonstrate activity that is neither joyful, angry, nor frightened. This response may be described as a nonemotional or a task-oriented behavior.

All individuals display these responses in their contact with the environment. Although each person displays every type of emotion, there are differences in emotional style which discriminate our three Relationship Styles from one another. The differences are not so much in the choice of emotion displayed, but in the frequency of displaying each emotion.

Let us be more specific for Directors, Accommodators and Isolators.

The Director

Directors who seek a sense of mastery and dominance over their environment tend to display two essential emotions in response to the world around them: happiness when they win or get their way, and anger when they don't. **Fear is not an emotion most Directors can easily access.** We have observed that it is very difficult for Directors to cry or display fear or helplessness. In order to assist the Director in accessing these emotions, a cathartic technique is usually necessary, one which creates an explosion of anger and then a release of sadness. This is known as Gestalt therapy and it is a technique that encourages emotional release.

A diagram may make this more understandable:
Director > frustrating event > blocked anger > sadness > therapist exaggerates anger > eventual discharge of sadness

> discharging sadness leads to relaxation or calming effect.

This scenario indicates the pattern utilized to help the Director release pent-up emotional blocks. **It is comfortable for the Director to lead with anger to cover up fear.** A psychologist once explained the essence of therapy as: "We aid the afflicted and afflict the aided." Essentially, this means that a Director needs an approach to break down the emotional defensiveness that prevents contact with more vulnerable aspects of his or her personality. A useful slogan for a Director may be, "Under each ounce of anger we may discover a pound of hidden sadness." In order to encounter this sadness, defenses need to be pried away. Directors are often resistant to change in therapy.

Lowen's Bioenergetics, which use physical exercises to break through blocked defenses, are often helpful to motivate a Director. The exercises involve a breathing technique and imagery work. These procedures aid a Director in getting beyond the mask of anger and into deeper parts of the mind. This type of therapy replaces the once-popular "primal therapy" technique. Primal therapy generally involved a lot of emoting and screaming that hoped to clean up the anger that often covers deep layers of sadness and vulnerability.

The Accommodator

The primary need of an Accommodator is to fit in and be accepted by others. Unlike Directors, they do not find anger an acceptable emotion with which to accomplish this goal. Accommodators' primary emotional reactions are happy and joyful when they fit in and are accepted, and fearful and overwhelmed when their sense of inclusion is threatened. Accommodators are often seen as people pleasers, unable to assert themselves for fear of alienating others.

Here is a case that illustrates this point. Janet is a 26-year-old woman, who is married and has two children, ages four and two. Her husband is an angry and intermittently substance-abusing carpenter. In therapy she describes a history of accelerating panic attacks. In the first session Janet cries, telling about her inability to receive any nurturing from her husband.

Let's diagram her dilemma to make it a more understandable one:

Accommodator > frustrating event > panic attack > blocked anger > therapist exaggerates patient's frustration > patient reaches impasse > eventually explodes > experiences sense of control and release of anxiety.

When under threat Accommodators become overwhelmed or flooded with fear. This fear prevents them from establishing an adult sense of control. In order to regain control their sense of power must be reconnected; this power is obscured by their lack of comfort with anger, and being assertive with their emotions.

Therapeutic work with Accommodators focuses on conquering fear and leaning to develop a sense of competency. Integrating blocked anger is an important step in accomplishing this goal for an Accommodator. **The inability to control one's sense of fear leads to accepting unhealthy relationships.** We have discussed how unhealthy Accommodators are prone to having abusive relationships. Uncovering anger, using it to set limits and demand better treatment is the

Accommodator's ultimate salvation to escape the cycle of emotional dependency and mistreatment. Janet is frightened by being alone, so she tolerates poor treatment. Her therapeutic task is to reencounter her blocked anger and assertively demand better treatment from her husband or to move out of her relationship if she does not receive better treatment. This movement is only possible if she can overcome her fear. By practicing what we described for Accommodators in Chapter 6, Janet is starting to make progress.

The Isolator

Isolators are not as clearly dominated by either fear or anger. They possess a subtle inability to encounter deeper emotional elements in themselves, which actually creates the isolation. Usually, the psychological defense mechanism known as "intellectualization" predominates in the life of the Isolator. Intellectualization is a way in which a person blocks out feelings by thinking. This basic defense mechanism accompanies the Isolator's way of being in the world. Both anger and fear create forms of contact. However, neither emotion is an ideal way in which to establish contact. By closing off much of their deeper emotional life, Isolators have become unavailable. This happens as the Isolator denies and suppresses his or her feelings. If they don't have to "feel," then they don't have to "deal" with it. This doesn't imply that Isolators don't experience anger or fear, but those emotions are filtered by defenses, primarily intellectualization, that allow them to ignore or reject their need for closeness. This pattern, established in early adulthood, creates a way of life that becomes increasingly more difficult to change as they get older.

Isolators refuse to fully experience their emotional needs, especially with a significant other. Here is an example of the Isolator's reaction to an emotional crisis:

> Steven, a 43-year-old businessman, is a wealthy bachelor who has had a series of long-term relationships, each of which he has sabotaged by withdrawing once the relationship is established. Steven is currently dating a younger woman who is deeply in love with him. Frustrated by his noncommittal attitude, she pushes him into therapy. After a few sessions, it becomes clear that Steven is not going to marry her, and, deeply hurt, she stops seeing him, probably hoping for an emotional reaction to assure her that he really does care.

Steven's reaction is to do nothing. He neither mourns nor pursues her. His unemotional comment, when confronted about their breakup, is, "She is a nice girl. We just want different things." **Steven's reaction lacks anger or sadness; it is devoid of emotion. This is a classic response of an Isolator in emotional crisis.** Steven is now free to pursue a new relationship. Inevitably it will demand a commitment that he is unwilling to give. Humans are creatures of patterns, and Isolators demonstrate behaviors that are decidedly predictable.

Many Isolators eliminate intimate relationships altogether as they get older. They adjust to living alone and develop friendships as substitutes for love. Isolators may seek therapy when their depression becomes severe, and they are not satisfied with their solitary existence. They seldom, however, demonstrate the full range of emotional expression in terms of anger, fear, and joy, which is noted in the other two Relationship Styles. In a way the isolation process involves a splitting apart of their emotional life, not only from others, but from themselves as well.

A review of the emotional lives of our three Relationship Styles:

*Directors tend to use anger as a primary way of responding when under emotional assault.
*Accommodators are vulnerable to being hurt and become overwhelmed with fear and sadness when under pressure.
*Isolators tend to reduce their emotional world to show less variety and intensity in their interpersonal lives.

The important question is: Can the emotional style of an individual be altered? For years doctors have relied on prescribed medication, often combined with psychotherapy, to control emotional extremes in individuals. Medication and psychotherapy do not, however, alter the underlying character of the individual. They do modify reactions that can be harmful to the individual or others. We believe that the first important step in changing an emotional style is to identify the Relationship Style and then acknowledge that we do act in a certain way based on this style. As we learn about ourselves, we use this knowledge to improve our emotional responses to others, which directly improves the quality of our relationships.

CHAPTER 9

MARRIAGE AND OTHER INTERESTING RELATIONSHIPS

In Chapter 1 we described the three basic stages through which relationships progress: a fantasy period, a reality period, and finally an accommodation phase. This chapter investigates how intimate relationships move through these stages. We give special attention to long-term committed relationships. We consolidate ideas about Relationship Style from previous chapters and integrate them with the topic of long-term relationship development.

Marriage, a basic ritual in all cultures, promotes procreation, maintains sexual mores and satisfies **everyone's basic need for intimate social involvement.** The institution of marriage has undergone its most radical transformation in the twentieth century. Until modern times many marriages were entered into mainly for economic or political reasons. Now "romantic love" is the primary reason for getting married. In addition, religious and racial limitations have become less restrictive, and divorce, while not a pleasant option, has lost most of its negative stigma.

More than half of all Americans who enter into marriage experience divorce. Few expect to be part of this statistic when they wed and none will tell you that divorce was a pleasant experience. But it is an option that allows couples to escape unhappy situations. Before they choose divorce as the solution, many couples often seek counseling from organized religious institutions, psychologists or marriage counselors. Each provide a unique source of insight and comfort.

We will now examine the stages of marriage and long-term relationships in detail. We will show how these stages are directly influenced by our three Relationship Styles.

The Fantasy Stage

Many of our beliefs about marriage, love, and sexuality are based on romantic literature, television, movies, popular music, and theatrical performances which shape our view of falling in love. These views are profoundly embedded in our culture and few can avoid them. However, our actual childhood experience (how we saw our parents relate) may be the complete opposite of our romantic image. Often the conflict in what we saw and what we want prevents couples from dealing effectively with the reality of a marriage relationship and can lead to divorce, adultery and remarriage.

The *fantasy stage* begins long before the first romantic contact. It consists of infatuation, crushes, and fantasies about unobtainable love objects such as movie stars or older, unavailable individuals such as teachers or counselors. Preadolescent and adolescent fantasies set the stage for our early love encounters. The mind-set of falling in love is similar for all three Relationship Styles. It is strong and pervasive. All

Directors, Accommodators, and Isolators internalize this mind-set. **Only after conflict arises in a relationship do we begin to see the marked differences between the three Relationship Styles in the way that they resolve problems.**

In the fantasy stage we are attracted to someone. We have a chemical erotic reaction; we are drawn to them. This attraction may last for a few months or even years. It leads to the beginning of romantic contact. (The fantasy of falling in love and finding someone who responds is critical to this stage.) Initially we know little about the inner person who is our new love. We only learn over time about their conflicts, childhood and relationship history that preceded our romance.

The fantasy stage is just as the name implies. It is usually an unrealistic arousal of romantic idealism and, physiologically, a sexual, erotic excitation. This stage can last a few days, one sexual encounter, or many years. **The fantasy essentially ends when conflicts appear and the illusion of perfection is destroyed.** For example, Sarah longs for John when at work. She is a attracted to his long hair and tanned skin. After a night of passion, she realizes the next morning that he only talks about and lives for surfing. She hates the water and the beach. She terminates the relationship at the fantasy stage.

In relationships that lead to commitment, the fantasy stage usually endures for a number of months and is accompanied by excessive romantic contact, regular sexual activities, or other regular forms of petting, kissing, or expressing affection. If the couple becomes engaged during the fantasy period, before they experience many disagreements or disappointments, they may delay experiencing the resolution of conflicts (knowledge about the way each resolves problems may in fact serve to prolong the fantasy). The engagement itself then leads to new fantasies and often extends this period of early love. Many couples marry long before the fantasy period is over. They make a long-term decision about their life without having read anything but the opening chapter of their novel.

The tendency toward premature coupling is especially common in teenagers and young couples. But the same impulsive behavior exists in individuals in their 40s, 50s, and 60s. Why the rush? **The eroticism of the fantasy period creates the illusion that the love needs to be grasped quickly or it will be lost forever.** Marriage fulfills a basic need in the relationship to possess the desired love object. **Accommodators rush to commitment faster than Directors or Isolators.** Marriage fulfills their most essential need for communion. **Isolators, during the fantasy period, often hold back or give mixed messages.** In this way, they often destroy a relationship out of their fear of committing to anyone. **Directors, during the fantasy stage, remain true to form, and do what they can to take control.** They resist relinquishing any power in the relationship. And when they do it is rarely without a conflict.

In summary, the fantasy stage is marked by a sense of newness and excitement. The day-to-day stressors of married life have yet to appear. The novelty has not faded, and the frequency of sexual eroticism **shields** the couple from viewing impending future conflicts and disappointments.

The Reality Phase and the Destruction of the Romantic Myth

Life happens, things change and the reality stage begins. As the initial excitement of the fantasy stage wears off, the buffer for our partner's habits can become thin and irritating. Often, squabbles, fights and misunderstandings are more frequent.

In short-lived relationships the reality phase usually comes abruptly. This happens with many Isolators whose boundaries are threatened. To escape the fear of commitment, Isolators can end a relationship without any explanation. Directors (ones who are self-centered or unprepared for long-term commitment) can also abandon a relationship during the reality stage without working through its concerns. These situations are not to be confused with the slow shift that occurs in marriage when a committed relationship encounters signs of trouble.

It is a rare relationship where the fantasy stage lasts forever, and where the initial infatuation doesn't eventually shift. We see this most often when two Accommodators marry. If neither is particularly controlling or isolating as a secondary trait, they may have a marriage with relatively little strife.

The majority of long-term relationships inevitably go through a reality phase that challenges the emotional resources of the couple. When this tears irreparably at the fabric of their commitment it results in the dissolution of the marriage or relationship. **Your Relationship Style affects the way you look at and act toward your partner and de-**

termines how, as a couple, you survive the reality phase.
There are some fairly predictable patterns we will outline to
illustrate how the reality stage proceeds.

Director Man - Unassertive, Accommodator Woman

The example of a Director man and an unassertive,
Accommodator woman is probably the most written about in
psychology. When this relationship is unhappy or unhealthy,
the term "codependent" is used to describe a woman willing
to tolerate mistreatment by an emotionally, physically, or
substance-abusing spouse.

A typical scenario: A couple is married after a brief
courtship. He hides a lot of his controlling or demanding style
during the fantasy stage of courtship. Enamored by his attention, she attempts to please him by showering him with
affection and frequent sex. Initially their relationship seems
blissful. Then the first blow-up occurs. He comes home irritable and criticizes how she cleans house. A pattern of criticizing and defending begins. If the husband was physically
abused as a child, it is likely their arguments may lead to
violence, especially if his wife is hysterical and emotionally
overreactive herself. She may, in fact, initiate the violence by
slapping or hitting her spouse when he is critical or berating.
Unfortunately, these violent transactions between Directors
and Accommodators are common. Violent domestic occur-
rences are found at all economic levels.

The problems arise because a Director will either criticize or attempt to improve his Accommodator partner. As an
Accommodator she will try to absorb his criticisms, ignoring

her own hurt feelings. This almost always leads to resentments. Resentment creates a sense of distance and disappointment. Unless hurt feelings are dealt with as they occur, the destruction of a relationship progresses. Counseling and communications training can provide struggling or unhappy couples a way to resolve conflicts effectively. Partners in a marriage need to learn to cope with their personal resentments, which if not dealt with properly eventually sabotage the relationship.

A violent interaction is the worse possible case for a Director and Accommodator in relationships. But there are many Director-Accommodator couples that are doing quite well. For these couples, a balance exists that allows them to live in peace and harmony in spite of their different styles.

Director Woman - Unassertive Accommodator Man

The stereotype of the Director Woman - Unassertive Accommodator Man is characterized by the overly assertive, bossy wife and the passive, submissive husband. The criticizing and demanding style of the Director woman can have a similar impact on the unassertive man. He may feel weak and inadequate, but have few tools with which to verbally spar with his more dominating wife. This type of relationship is frequently depicted on television and in films. Although sometimes comical in films, the true story often reflects the painful side to the Director Woman and Accommodator Man relationship.

Some cultures are more matriarchal, both socially and politically. Here the relationship pattern of the domineering female is more customary. In southern Mexico there's a town called Tehuantepec where women control the marketplace and the men are quite subservient. Here one might find a direct proposition from a woman to be the norm. In most Western cultures, however, the trend has been patriarchal, with the males in the dominating positions, both socially and politically. The social history of the United States has shown this until recently. The acceptance of women in roles of power and authority is growing, albeit slowly. With this, there is a further acceptance of the Director Woman - Accommodator Man Relationship Style union. Resistance to this type of relationship alliance is found in traditional religious and politically conservative groups.

In reality, many Director wife - Accommodator husband relationships are successful, if a certain balance is established that meets the needs of both partners. Some people want to lead and others to follow. Males do not have a monopoly on leadership when it comes to the inner workings of the family.

Gay and Lesbian Relationships

Most gay and lesbian relationships have similar issues. In our practice we have noted that there are few unique characteristics of gay and lesbian couples when it comes to Relationship Style combinations. Most gay and lesbian couples are similar to straight couples in regard to communication and transactional patterns. One frequent example is a couple of similar age with self-sufficient incomes. Another common pattern is the older Director paired with the much younger

Accommodator. Remember, the important factor is the character of the individual, not sexual orientation. The important defining factor is how you treat your partner and how he or she treats you. **Love, commitment, honor and respect do not depend upon gender or sexual orientation.** Understanding your Relationship Style gives you the tools to make accommodations and improvements.

Director Man - Director Woman

Romantic relationships between two Directors either crash and burn fast, or provide a challenging environment in which both parties are forced to grow. There is seldom anything in between. To be successful two Directors must learn the limits of their power and how to avoid controlling each other.

In a hypothetical case a couple both score high for Director, but have an elevated Accommodation score. This couple's needs are a mixture of a desire for control, as well as a countering need for love and affiliation. Remember, Directors try to control their environment in order not to feel fear. A loved one is part of this environment. Although this couple will argue and frustrate each other, they can resolve the issues of the reality phase and remain married for many years. A Director with a healthy attitude toward commitment and marriage will be most likely to survive the challenges of the reality phase. Directors who perceive individuals as replaceable may be unable to work through the discouraging moments of this period. Issues that weigh heavily in the success or failure of Director-Director marriages or relationships are whether they are prone to adultery as a solution to their boredom and frustration, and how they saw their same sex parent act in relationships.

A painful reality in many marriages is that most of the disturbed behaviors of our parents will come back to haunt us. Much of what our years of therapy have taught us about human beings is that the unconscious role model our parents provide directly affects on our adult behavior. The reason why we are so influenced by what we see our parents do may be as simple as modeling: a baby duck following its mother. It may be as complex as genetics. The complex interactions between modeling, genetics and birth order are so powerful that by adolescence, most Relationship Styles are established. A question one needs to ask is: **Does your Relationship Style work for you and create order in your life or does your Relationship Style work against you and order your life around?** The answer to this should become more apparent as we continue.

Isolators

With an Isolator's essential need for distance, we find that marriages are a compromise at best. When Isolators fall in love, they can easily be enrolled in the fantasy phase of love and marriage. This is especially true in early adulthood before the pattern of relationship sabotage and isolation is well established. Isolators generally have difficulty expressing feelings in a direct and acceptable manner. Some may actually have a biological urge to maintain their separateness. A combination of these factors may keep Isolators from marrying. Isolators will almost always need to learn to negotiate the day-to-day problems effectively. When Isolators marry, many find the constraints of marriage unworkable. Those marriages tend to collapse quickly, statistically in less than 18 months.

A successful Isolator marriage is usually one where the Isolator can retain a relative emotional distance without upsetting his or her spouse. It breaks down when a dependent Accommodator is afraid to leave an unavailable and distant Isolator. Some Isolators, concerned about their difficulties in marriage, will cooperate with their frustrated spouses and accept the need for marital counseling; unfortunately a great number refuse. They would rather end a long-term relationship than directly face the frustration felt by their spouse. Only a cooperative Isolator can alter his or her behavior. Marriage counseling or psychotherapy that includes a focus on improving communication skills is a great advantage in the success of an Isolator relationship.

The Accommodation Phase: The Key to Relationship Longevity

Relationships are dynamic. This means that they are constantly changing and partners are forced to adjust to the change. After the fantasy stage ends and the challenges of the reality period begin, new adjustments must be made for a marriage to endure. These adjustments can be referred to as the *accommodation phase*. Accommodation is a way in which couples cope with the imperfections of marital life. Prob-

lems sometimes are not completely resolved with accommodation. Power struggles, communication difficulties, and general dissatisfaction from the loss of the fantasy phase can be
worked on and accepted.

Key factors in this phase of the relationship are:

* How your parents showed you what to expect.
* Economics.
* Communication style.
* Health and lifestyle.
* Your Relationship Style.
* Both partner's commitment to making it work.

**The unique interaction of these factors in a rela-
tionship will determine the marriage's survival.**

How your parents showed you what to expect. The
manner in which your parents dealt with discord and how
they resolved problems will have a powerful unconscious
impact on your ability to make adjustments during the accommodation phase.

Economic and financial factors can be a major stressors and have undermining impact on the foundation of your
relationships. Too often these types of stressors lead to the
end of relationships that would have otherwise survived.

Communication patterns established early in the
marriage can either enhance problem solving or lead to the
ultimate demise of the marriage.

Lifestyle compatibility helps relationships survive
better when the couple have common shared interests, for
example, going to the gym or health club, traveling together,
going to the theater, enjoying music together and sharing
mutual friendships. These compatible interests become more

relevant once the passion of the fantasy period has subsided.

Making a commitment to a healthy lifestyle is easier when you have partner with similar goals. This includes your approach to nutrition, exercise, relaxation, sleeping patterns, idle time and sex (not necessarily in this order).

Understanding your personal Relationship Style and your partner's style will affect your relationship. We stress the importance of understanding the concept of Relationship Styles in leading to healthier, stronger and more effective relationships.

Both partners need to be committed to making the marriage work. A shared positive attitude toward making the marriage work will only help your marriage. **"It takes two people to make a marriage, but only one person to end one."**

There are two distinctly different outcomes to the accommodation phase. One is a healthy recommitment to the relationship. Differences are acknowledged and the couple works to continue the love and joy in spite of them. The other type of accommodation is much less positive. The couple stays together in a relationship that neither enjoys. Usually this is a direct result of economic interdependence and habit. **All accommodations in marriage lead to the acceptance of the relationship, for better or worse.**

Healthy relationships demand that the partners be willing to confront their childhood programming, their Relationship Style and their communication style to avoid repeating negative patterns that create unhappiness. This will make a difference in your marriage.

A Director who is willing to accept his or her controlling behavior, and is willing to work on ways of changing some of the relationship's more destructive elements, is distinctly different from a Director who refuses therapy and blames his or her spouse for the marital difficulty. Key to relationship survival is each individual's willingness to be open and honest about these issues. It might be instinct or human nature, but we often learn to blame others for their essential lack of completeness. In this way we are prevented from facing the truth about ourselves. The truth is that we are responsible for our own choices. This includes who we marry and how we react to that choice during our marriage.

Our Relationship Styles dictate many of the terms that control the progress of our long-term relationships. **Accommodators tend to appease their spouses.** When this appeasing process is not fulfilled or reciprocated the result is often the accumulation of resentment. Learning to be more balanced and less accommodating is key in preventing the **unconscious** sabotaging of a marriage.

This is equally true for an Accommodator married to a Director, or an Accommodator married to an Isolator. In either scenario, the Accommodator is confronted with a sense of being abandoned. In an Accommodator-Director marriage, the sense of emotional abandonment is frequently caused by feeling criticized and discounted. In an Accommodator-Isolator union, it is more a sense of rejection and emotional abandonment that pervades the Accommodator's sense of loss. In order to prevent these factors from eventually destroying the foundation of the marriage, Accommodators seek balance in learning to assert themselves. They need to request that their spouse work on their behavior in order to prevent the accumulation of anger in the Accommodator. **Accommodators need to use words such as "I want," "I need," and "I require" more often.** In this way they can attempt to get their needs met and avoid feeling that they come second in the marriage.

Directors in a marriage relationship are challenged to balance their need for domination and control. They must recognize this need or they will eventually alienate a healthy spouse. Directors, as indicated in earlier chapters, tend to overuse the parental aspect of their personality. They tend to give orders and advice too freely. They often criticize when their directions are not followed closely. At worst, unhealthy Directors show violent and abusive tendencies, which destroy any emotional bonding with their spouses. Unhealthy Directors also <u>blame others</u> for the problems that occur in their long-term relationships. A recognition of one's controlling tendencies and a willingness to modify them through negotiation are necessary to resolve the "angry parent" or "resentful child" interaction patterns frequently seen in Director-Accommodator or Director-Isolator marriages. Communications training offers alternative techniques for expressing one's needs. <u>One easy and simple</u> exercise is just to use the words "we" and "I" in describing an issue, rather than "you." This can greatly reduce feelings of resentment caused by a criticizing or dominating spouse. For example:

(Negative pattern) *He*: You should stop charging things on your Visa card.

She: You do it, too.

(Positive pattern) *He*: I'd like us to work together and pay off our credit card debt and try to prevent it from resurfacing.

She: What do you suggest?

Remember that words are powerful triggers. Directors need to be aware of how their critical comments affect their spouse's feelings. They have to look at the communication patterns they have already established. Patterns are ingrained and illustrate childhood learning acquired by modeling our parents. Because we have used them for a long time, it may be difficult to change them, <u>but not impossible</u>. Commitment to the process of change is essential for a couple that wants to improve the quality of their intimate life together. The pay-off is, of course, a good and healthy relationship.

Isolators in long-term relationships have already succeeded in breaking their basic pattern of withdrawing and sabotaging emotional commitments. The near physical proximity of Isolators with their spouse, however, does not imply that the behavioral pattern has been eliminated. Isolators in marriage relationships may show unhealthy patterns of withdrawing; limited verbal, physical, as well as sexual contact. Over time this undermines the marriage and attacks the commitment of their spouse. To improve their relationships Isolators must acknowledge their Relationship Style and realize the impact isolating can have on a loved one. Then they must discuss issues openly with their spouse and listen to the other's feelings about being left out.

An example of a negative model:

She: I want to go to the movies tonight. Would you take me?

He: I'm developing film in my darkroom and need to

have them done by tomorrow.

She: You haven't taken me to a movie in over six months.

He: (Silence, ending the discussion. This was an unconscious way for him to say: "Leave me alone."

And an example of a positive model:

He: Honey, I took the Relationship Assessment Scale. Looks like I am an Isolator. Do you feel I am an Isolator?

She: Yes. You spend a lot of time alone, and I seldom know how you feel, whether you really want to spend time with me.

He: I do want to be with you. I just don't know what to talk about. After awhile I just pull back. I guess I have always been this way.

In the first example a negative dialogue shows an interaction that leads the wife to feel rejected and unimportant. It also shows how an Isolator retreats. In the second and positive example, there is an open dialogue between the couple. It also demonstrates self-exploration which can lead to mutual acceptance by the couple. Isolators must also be willing to understand their behavior and be committed to changing it. Even small changes can have a major impact on a relationship. Isolators who challenge themselves can improve their relationships.

We have presented the different phases in the development of long-term relationships. The Relationship Style is a very important tool in understanding how our communication patterns with another person develop over time. We have explained how the interactions of our Relationship Styles either strengthen or weaken a long-term commitment. Learning to resolve problems together is an important key to the longevity of any relationship. **The ability to empathize, in other words, to see and feel what your partner is experiencing, is probably the most important ingredient in an intimate, happy and successful relationship.**

CHAPTER 10

HELPING PARENTS DEVELOP HEALTHY CHILDREN

Understanding Relationship Styles helps parents develop healthy children. The interaction between your inherited temperament and birth order, as well as your role in your family, has significant impact on what you will become in terms of your Relationship Style. Think back a moment about the way you were as a child. What was your position and role in your family? Were you the oldest who was made responsible for your younger siblings by your parents? Were you the baby, pampered by older parents to whom you represented their last opportunity at youth and parenting? Possibly you were a middle child whose role was never well defined, and you struggled to establish a sense of identity and position in your family.

The combination of genetic predisposition, birth order, and family factors creates the raw material for character formation. The unknown genetic factor, which is referred to as "nature," plays a critical role in the development of our early childhood personalities. Parents can describe distinct factors in their toddlers that differentiate them from their siblings. For instance, John likes to read all day, while Jake likes to climb trees. Do you remember how your parents described your personality?

Just as important is the issue of imitating parental style. This is unique to all individuals and only partially explainable. It is the basis for the creation of childhood personality and eventually Relationship Style. Children can idolize their parents and assimilate those traits and attributes into their own personality. **Or just the opposite.** They may develop very different personality characteristics of their parents in rebellion.

We will now look at the three types of Relationship Styles as they appear in childhood.

The Isolator Child

The Isolator child rarely plays with peers. He or she may be lonely or may just like to be alone. These children are not usually disruptive and therefore do not find themselves in counseling as often as others that are unruly. These are children whose temperament may be introverted and they are often slow to talk. When these children have parents that are not actively involved in their lives, their adolescent years are marked with increased rates of depression and suicide attempts. Children who spend years in boarding schools without frequent interaction with their parents often become victims of this type of isolation. But any emotional or physical neglect breeds feelings of loneliness and leads these children to isolate themselves, setting up the way in which they tend to relate to others in adulthood. They in effect isolate themselves from pain, disappointment, and sadness. The most effective therapy with individuals who isolate themselves and become detached emotionally is that which maintains or creates a sense of security in an intimate relationship.

The Accommodator Child

Western culture is fast to applaud the child who joins the mainstream of activities. Movies, television and organized religion reinforce that it is good to be with others, to fall in love, to participate in school clubs and activities, to join the team and play sports. These activities are valued and considered healthy. The child who fits into these activities is "okay." While being social is a sign of being well adjusted, children who are unable to play alone or be by themselves are considered not well adjusted. Accommodators, who are afraid of being alone and who lack assertiveness when dealing with others, often are candidates for early sexual activity, alcohol and drug abuse and poor peer associations in an attempt to fit in somewhere. Accommodators whose desire to please others outweighs their own ability to choose activities that are good for them benefit from therapies that develop a sense of self.

The Director Child

As a child, the Director is often seen attempting to control his or her environment by trying to control others. When Director children are well adjusted, they have a strong sense of fair play as well. They can temper a strong will or dominant personality by fulfilling their need for power through achievement. This happens in socially accepted behaviors such as excelling in academics or participating in leadership roles in school or the community. On the other hand, children who like to direct and are out of control behaviorally may have trouble sharing or waiting their turn. At worst, this child is a bully who dominates others in an angry and violent manner.

Director children are a product of their genetics, birth order and family experience, in the same way that the Accommodators and Isolators are affected. In an unhealthy environment, Directors are desperately trying to gain some power in their life when they feel they have none. Abused children act out aggressively to try to regain control and avoid being victimized in the only way they have seen, by abusing others. In more appropriate homes, the Director may be the oldest child who has experienced a sense of mastery over siblings and has developed a strong need for assertiveness. When this trait is nurtured, these children can become leaders in their own right.

The Balancing Act

Understanding your child's unique character will help him or her achieve a sense of balance between the need or desire to direct, accommodate or isolate. **THE HEALTHY ADULT CAN DRAW FROM ANY OF THESE STYLES AND NOT RELY ON JUST ONE.** Your child's ability to balance the use of these styles comes from developing a sense of autonomy and self-esteem and from learning to respect the rights of others.

The Relationship Assessment Scale, however, was not intended to be used in assessing the relationship tendencies of children or adolescents. While several psychological tests are used to measure a child's intelligence, academic achievement and personality functioning, behavioral observation may best assess their style of interaction. Here are some simple techniques to do just that.

What to Look For

After you determine your child's Relationship Style, we will give you some basic techniques and skills to help guide your child's behavior toward a more balanced style.

To study your child's interactions with others, simply look at the way he or she plays with other children. Does your child try to dominate all play activity, or like to play only with older or younger children? Follow the leader more than offer leadership? Act more assertive or more withdrawn in interactions with others? The answers to these questions will give you a clue to your child's developing Relationship Style.

Because your child may act differently around you than with others, it is important to get feedback from other people. Ask those who are in contact with your child or teen to tell you how they view your child's interaction and social performance. This includes your neighbors, parents of your child's friends or playmates and teachers. Talking with teachers about your child's social as well as academic performance is important and valuable. Modern education is constantly trying to improve the methods of teaching the whole child. In most cases the people entrusted with your child's education

are very concerned about the emotional and social development of your child, as well as academic performance.

The parents of your child's (and especially your teen's)
friends are a valuable source of information about behavior
when you are not present. Additionally, they are an important source of support. Knowing the parents of your child's
friends allows you greater insight into the peer group and its
pressures. It provides you allies to establish appropriate behavior guidelines and build trust.

Talk with your child. Talk with your spouse. Listen to
your other children and friends regarding your son or
daughter's social behavior. Have regular family meetings,
especially when one parent is absent due to work demands
or because of divorce.

Remember that parents' Relationship Style will trans-
fer to their children. People who present a balanced approach
to life generally pass on these traits to their children. But do
not panic if you or your spouse (current or not) displays an
unbalanced Relationship Style. Be fair to yourself (and your
loved ones). In cases where divorce or separation has divided
families, children face greater risks. This is true concerning
all types of emotional and behavioral acting out. Not all children or adolescents of troubled parents will display emotional
or behavioral problems, but there is a greater chance of that
due to their experiences of instability.

But in the same way, parents who are balanced in their
Relationship Styles should not ignore these interactional patterns in their children. All young people are vulnerable. People
who tend to function in a more balanced fashion should be
aware of where their children are in their social development.

The balanced Director father and balanced Accommodator or Isolator mother are more likely to continue to look after their child's needs regardless of their own personal problems or losses. This is generally true for all three balanced Relationship Styles. Even married couples with balanced Relationship Styles will sometimes have problems that cannot be resolved short of separation or divorce. Balance in Relationship Style always allows people, whether Director, Isolator, or Accommodator, to conduct themselves appropriately around their children when faced with these difficult situations. Children will adapt to the changes brought on by stressful life events such as divorce, death, or remarriage of a parent. These issues along with problems centered around a poor relationship with a brother, sister, stepbrother or stepsister can also affect the way a child's Relationship Style will develop.

When a parent is a Director, there is often a dictatorial pattern in communication within the family. A need for power and control will suppress a child's ability to express him or herself adequately, resulting in negative self-image or affiliations. On the other hand, when an Isolator parent is the primary caretaker, the child is often given too much leeway in deciding how to relate to others. With Accommodator parents, the child's level of individualism may be suppressed. This often creates conflicts in emotions, especially when the child may desire to take a more balanced approach. An example of this is in families where the parents have secrets which are never to be questioned by the maturing child or teenager.

The maturity of the parents is another important factor in the emotional experience of the child. A child who has already developed a strong character type in his or her personality, identity, temperament or Relationship Style will respond in ways expected of his or her developmental level. When families experience a nasty divorce, where the parents are inappropriately acting out, the children's behavior will often reflect this. When parents act out, their kids will also act out. Too often there is a push away from a balanced style. This is readily observed in the Accommodator child who displaces his or her family with friends. At the extreme this is the child who becomes affiliated with gangs. Even when gangs are not a problem, this type of child will sometimes affiliate with other troubled peers. The need to be accepted is so great that this child will often go against his or her own better judgment. Accommodators will push away, looking to join others, gangs at worst, high achieving peer groups at best.

The Director child's need to dominate, especially when his or her parents have problems, will often produce an overdemanding youth and in some cases a bully. An Isolator, whose tendency is to withdraw, will sometimes be identified as the child who "falls through the cracks." This type of child often goes unnoticed until it is too late. The child may continue to perform adequately academically, but emotionally the seeds may have been planted for emotional disturbance. Most notably, these youngsters are prone to developing a mood disorder such as depression. Please seek professional help if you think that your child is developing or experiencing depression.

When children act out their emotional conflicts through their behavior, knowing your child's Relationship Style will help you identify the <u>severity</u> of the problem. The Director's need to dominate may become out of control and unmanageable. The Accommodator may turn away from potentially helpful advice and rules. The Isolator child or teen may become even more withdrawn from family and peers.

Sibling interaction can also be very important. Your child's relationships (balanced or unbalanced) with brothers or sisters reflects significantly the way he or she may be responding to others outside the family. As a parent, whether you are married, separated, divorced, or widowed, it is important to establish balance in the roles and rules you create for your family. Set standards for the way you want your family to communicate both inside and outside of the home.

Divorce

The process for creating and maintaining a healthy, balanced child is not impossible if the parents divorce. It just becomes more challenging. Divorce is emotionally draining, even when the marriage is over and one or both partners experience relief from all the stress. Divorce creates changes in lifestyle that often limit a parent's ability to address all of the important things required to ensure a healthy environment for the child.

THE BASIC RULES FOR A HEALTHY FAMILY ENVIRONMENT

The following are simple guidelines to provide a positive, balanced family environment:

* **Define and clarify the roles each person has in your family.**
* **Establish rules that act as guidelines to live by.**
* **Have a system of rewards and consequences that is understood by all family members.**
* **Promote open communications within the family.**
* **Express love, warmth and commitment!**

Establish and clarify the roles in your family. Simply, this means that parents need to act parental. Ideally, husband and wife should respond to one another with respect and all children should be allowed to grow up in a warm, safe and nurturing environment. This directly affects the development of the child's identity and his or her adult Relationship Style. As we stated before, providing healthy relationship models are just as important when parents are separated or divorced. Parents need to use their authority to reel in an overcontrolling child. A child who takes on the role of a parent, either with an adult or a sibling, is not living in a balanced home. A child should be encouraged to act age-appropriately in regard to behavior with others (including brothers and sisters). **Demonstrating effective and positive parenting role models will be reflected in the way your children respond later on to their own challenges as spouses and parents. If you demonstrate a positive, healthy, and balanced Relationship Style, your children will too.**

It is important to establish rules in your family. For a family to be effective, children need guidance and limits. Talk about what is acceptable and what is not with your children. Clearly define each person's responsibility in the family. This will help them achieve a more balanced approach. This should include the basics, such as bedtime rituals, dinnertime etiquette, guidelines for resolving problems and conflicts.

Follow through with both rewards and consequences for acceptable and inappropriate behavior. In this way your child will learn to take responsibility for his or her actions. Praise your child for doing well. Let children know when they are astray and follow through with fair and effective consequences. Clarify the rewards and consequences in advance. For example, choice of video rental when all chores are completed, or 30 minutes of time-out for fighting with a sibling. This way there should be few surprises. Save the surprises for birthdays and holidays. Try to be as consistent as you can. Studies show children respond in a positive way to consistency. While setting limits on negative behavior, remember it is equally important to reward good behavior. It is important for children to know they are doing the right thing.

Communicate, communicate, communicate! Keep the door of communication open in the family. Set limits for a controlling child. A controlling Director-type child needs an assertive and empathetic parent to harness the child's need to dominate. Encourage Accommodators to express their own views. An Accommodator needs clarification and support to see both sides of situations and to develop a sense of fairness. Teach Isolators to assert themselves. An Isolator child needs to know that it is safe to express feelings without fear of retribution. To do this take a calm and reflective stance with your child. Speak directly to him or her, not while doing some other chore like putting away the groceries or while watching television. Practice and use the "People Skills" that we describe later in this chapter.

Express love, warmth, and commitment to your child. Make family life a safe, comfortable, and nurturing experience. Take time to explore and discuss issues and problems. Offer encouragement and express pride in accomplishment. This is very important for any of the three Relationship Styles. We have all heard the saying "An apple a day keeps the doctor away." Here is a new twist to an old theme: "A hug a day will keep the therapist away!" It has been well documented that children need to be hugged. The touch by a loving and caring parent can go far in reassuring your child. It is good for the mind, body and soul. Science has documented humans' need to be touched by others in a caring manner. It is so important that a child experience this form of genuine and healthy human contact. Hugging your children will help them develop into healthier and less neurotic adults.

People Skills

For younger children it is important for the parent to instill the basics of "people skills." These include social skills, communication skills, anger management, problem solving and what we call feeling skills.

Social skills focus on the development of good communications. The basics include such things as making eye contact with others when engaged in conversation. For an Isolator child whose insecurity is often overwhelming in social interactions, this is a very useful skill. A little Isolator boy once blurted out in a group session that this was "magic," as he showed his surprise at how effective this tool was in gaining the attention of others. He was even more pleased with the resulting ways in how others responded directly to him.

Demonstrate the proper distance to stand with others when engaging in conversation: approximately a "hand shakes" distance. An Accommodator child who was prone to silliness, often to gain the negative attention he sought (because for some children any attention, whether positive or negative, is a cry for their need to be accepted), profoundly responded when demonstrating proximity during conversing. He stated, "Give me the news, not the weather." He found that too close contact often resulted in a peer spraying him with saliva.

A cornerstone of communications theory suggests using "I" statements. This entails repeating or rephrasing what the other person said. It goes something like this: "John, I hear you say that you do not want to do your homework now because the cartoon show that is on is very important to you. Is that right?" The child then has to respond, either affirming that you understood his intention or further explaining himself. Notice that his name was used. This is a very important communication skill that when used with eye contact and "I" statements creates the "magic" that was described earlier. **It commands attention and builds respect. It also teaches empathy.**

Of course, using proper language is important and should be part of the family rules. Cursing or improper slang should be discouraged. The loudness or softness of a person's voice should be in accordance with proximity to the other person. A shy Isolator may need encouragement to speak up. Conversely, a Director child who is overly loud needs to be taught restraint.

All of these social skills are part of what we describe as "people skills." All children need to develop a basic knowledge and working understanding of these concepts to function effectively. People skills should be taught early, but it is never too late to start.

Anger management and problem solving go hand in hand. One of the underlying emotions that young people (or people of any age, for that matter) experience is frustration. Frustration without proper outlet may result in negative displays of emotions and behaviors. A Director child may increase the display of dominance, while an Accommodator may again go along with the crowd. Isolators may intensify their feelings of inadequacy and pull further away. Anger increases stress levels and impedes rational thinking and responses. Understanding and helping modify your child's response to anger will go a long way in their developing a balanced Relationship Style and healthy transition into adulthood. We discuss how to help your child cope with anger and frustration next.

DEALING WITH FIGHT OR FLIGHT

Often when a child resolves conflict, he or she is most likely to respond in what we have all heard of as "flight or fight." He or she will "run from it" or "stand and fight" about it. Most adults know there are other ways of resolving conflicts. The type of physical response chosen is integrated into

the thinking process. It is most apparent when a child must resolve a conflict. That is why anger management and problem-solving skills go together. By learning stress reduction techniques, a child's physical responses to stress (this includes anger and frustration) lessen and a more relaxed and clear-minded approach to problem solving is developed.

ACT

A simple technique to help a child refocus when angry or impeded by any emotion is called Attention Control Training or ACT.

This simple technique was designed by psychologist Robert Nideffer from his experience with self-hypnosis and martial arts. It was initially used to enhance athletic performance. It has been adapted specifically for children. The basic premise is that the body and mind cannot be in both a relaxed state and a tense state at the same time. To create a relaxed state the child stands and takes three successive, deep, diaphragmatic breaths (called "belly breaths" for youngsters). While doing this the child stands with the feet at shoulder distance apart, with one leg (right-handed, right leg; left-handed, left leg) just a few inches in front of the other leg and knees bent slightly. This helps create a more balanced position. The child takes the three "belly breaths" while pushing the weight downward. While doing this the child is instructed to think of a very special place, a place where he or she feels most relaxed, safe, and comfortable, such as the beach, at home in front of a fireplace, at the edge of a stream, or in front of a beautiful waterfall. The child is now more relaxed, balanced and receptive.

How It Works

The rhythmic breathing is a cornerstone of most forms of relaxation training. The mental image evokes peace, calm, and focus. The downward shift of weight increases balance and lessens the tension of the upper extremities when a person experiences stress. A child practiced in this skill may find it useful in many situations. Frustration and anger increase bodily stress and quickly reduce physical and thinking effectiveness. Using ACT prior to a sporting event or dreaded book report in front of a class can and will improve performance.

In situations where a child is bordering on losing control because of anger, ACT can help the child regain self-control and increase the likelihood of responding more appropriately. This is a good tool to help teach children to be assertive and not aggressive. Assertiveness allows one to stay in control of one's emotions, while being aggressive is acting out one's hostility. This works well for bullies or manipulators. It is equally as important for Isolators who hold everything in until they feel as if they will explode.

Being assertive and not aggressive is a very useful concept to teach children. But it helps to know the child's unique Relationship Style to understand in which direction to prompt him or her. To act, Isolators need to be drawn out of their shell, while Directors may need containment. Accommodators may find both encouragement and restraint effective depending on their situation.

When anger and frustration are managed, problem solving can be effective. **Remember, the fight or flight syndrome directly affects and often impedes the ability to solve problems effectively.** The reason is simple. When in fight or flight mode your body just responds and you don't "think." The response becomes reduced to two options, good or bad, black or white, true or false, hit little Johnny or run away. In a calm, reflective state a child has more control over him or herself and has increased levels of attention. Here more effective problem-solving strategies may be used.

Success with ACT has been phenomenal. Even if it sounds a little strange at first, it is very simple and effective. When practiced and rehearsed ACT can be accomplished in just a few moments anytime and anywhere.

The SODA Technique

A great technique for improving problem solving is called *SODA*. This stands for Situation Options Decision and Actions. Any problem can be described as a situation: for instance, which television show to watch, what to eat for dinner. Options are the choices we think of. Notice that options is in the plural form. Always encourage the child to create three or more options to address the situation, to break free of the stress response's grip on the thinking process. This will allow for a more rational and appropriate response to the situation. During a stressful encounter the thought process becomes tense. Thus, the fight or flight stress response often constricts an individual's ability to reason effectively. With teeth and fists clenched, a young person cannot think clearly and respond appropriately. Reduce this tension and allow the child time to select more options; then positive results are more likely to result.

Not all options are positive. It is important for a child to know this. All relevant options should be explored with the child, both good and bad. In this way a child begins to learn how to evaluate the results of different behaviors. The decision step in the SODA paradigm creates a process of evaluating the results of each possible option. For instance, in an encounter with another child in a schoolyard, a child may have to choose between several responses to a situation that can have a significant impact. A child in conflict may want to hit the other child; choose to walk away; or talk to a teacher or playground attendant. **Children must be taught that they are not limited in their initial responses**. In the above scenario a Director type may tend to act out frustration via physical contact or by badgering a teacher. An unbalanced Accommodator may choose to go along with whatever social pressures dictate. A more balanced Accommodator child may recognize the futility in the situation and just walk away. An Isolator child may take similar action as a balanced Accommodator, but instead of letting go of the experience of frustration may feel rejected and experience low self-esteem. This third step of the SODA technique, decision, requires that the individual think and weigh the best option for solving the current problem.

The last step in our problem-solving technique is action. Action is putting the option into a behavior. It may be useful to teach the youngster that actions equal behavior. Behavior is what people judge other people by. This is very simple and very true. The way a person behaves is what others observe and what they respond to.

With teenagers who may have conflicts with their parents, SODA may provide a useful tool to enhance communications. A central developmental component of adolescence is the ability to establish trust in relationships. Building trust starts with the family. Trust often diminishes when a parent and a teenaged child are at odds over problems they may be experiencing. Therefore, it is necessary in families with adolescents to teach the teen to negotiate effectively. Negotiating is only problem solving with two or more parties. SODA is an easy and useful technique that can provide a structured format for resolving many different types of conflicts.

Feeling Skills

What may be the most important part of developing your child's people skills are what we refer to as "feeling skills." "Feeling skills" come from our human qualities of empathy and sympathy. Empathy is what allows us to experience what another person is feeling, while sympathy is the expression of that concern. We have all heard of the term "a mother's intuition," a process where a mother can sense something about her child. Intuition has not been proven scientifically, but it has not been disproved either. We all have seen or heard of stories where a parent has some feeling about what is about to befall their child in advance or in concurrence with an event. It sounds mystical but there may be more to it. When a mother (or father) has an "intuition" it may reflect an advanced form of unconsciously applying empathy. Intuition may be thought of as a skill a parent develops over time and through contact with their child. It happens with anyone you spend a lot of time with. This is a skill that can be developed with practice. Stay alert to your mind and body's response to those around you. Take notice of the time, place, setting and environment. You might even try practicing yoga or meditation. People who practice these disciplines report greater awareness and insight along with the positive results that it provides the body. When you are more aware of what you are feeling and alert to the feelings of others you have increased your sensitivity. This sensitivity is what "feeling skills" are about.

No matter what your child's style is, your relationships will only improve by increasing sensitivity and expressing concern towards others. These are best demonstrated by the love, kindness and tolerance that parents show their child.

CHAPTER 11

YOUR RELATIONSHIP STYLE IN THE WORKING WORLD

We will now explore how your Relationship Style affects your choice of career and success in the workplace. The choice of vocation is probably one of the key developmental tasks of life. The manner in which an individual translates childhood fantasies of being a firefighter, police officer, doctor, or basketball star into a place in the working world is affected by our interests, abilities, and relationships. **This chapter will address two things; first, the Relationship Style we use at work with our supervisors and peers, and second, whether Directors, Isolators, and Accommodators are destined, by the nature of their characters, to be attracted to certain careers. Said another way: Some Relationship Styles are more successful in working with "things" rather than "people."** This chapter provides some general vocational themes to assist readers who are unsure of what career to choose or who are considering a mid-life change of career.

Relationship Style Is One of the Key Variables in Career Choice

Career choice is one of the key issues of early adulthood. For some, the choice of career involves a long-term goal which is realized after years of study and effort. For others, career choice is far less focused. Many people just fall into a career based on economic necessity, opportunity, or chance.

Numerous variables decide what career opportunities are available. Directors are poorly suited for a job in which subordination and obedience to authority is essential. Accommodators are likely to try their best to fit in any working situation. And an Isolator is very unlikely to run for political office. Successful vocational guidance has always attempted to match an individual's intelligence, personality, and interests to a satisfying occupation. **Because Relationship Style is a powerful aspect of personality it distinguishes many areas of interest and potential vocational choices.**

The First Choice: Working with People or Working with Things

Certain individuals are better suited to working in careers that have a lot of people contact, and some people are better off in jobs where there is limited interaction with people. These are careers frequently sought by Accommodators, Directors, or a combination of both. Isolators are not prone to choose a career that requires a lot of social involvement. This is not to say that an Isolator will not choose such a career. It will just take more adjustment for this type of person.

Jobs that stress working with people are social, human-centered, and involve extensive human interaction. Examples of these types of jobs are sales, social work, teaching, and law. Jobs more focused on working with things are tasks such as pharmacist, engineer, accountant, and carpenter. These are occupations in which human contact is a secondary aspect of the job. Extroverted individuals are drawn to social occupations, and introverted individuals are more happier in product work environments. Therefore, one may assume that Isolators would be predisposed to product-oriented work, and Accommodators to work with people. Directors are often split between occupational choices that allow them social leadership positions and those that allow them independence and autonomy. **It is the interaction between these Relationship Styles, as well as character style, that guides an individual's ultimate career choice.**

For example, there are teachers who are Accommodators, who primarily want to be accepted and fit in, and teachers who are Directors, who primarily want to be in control. At times, there are instructors who are Isolators, who adjust to the social demands of their jobs. On the other hand, few Accommodators would be vocationally satisfied with work as a research chemist for a large chemical company, where the primary job responsibility leaves them alone in a lab much of the time. A highly educated, introverted individual with an Isolator profile may be more uniquely suited for that career.

Since few Accommodators are satisfied with product-oriented work, they are best satisfied in an organized environment. Accommodators can, in fact, seek leadership positions in companies if they also have high levels of Director in their Relationship Style. Accommodators in the working world are usually dedicated employees who, if treated fairly, will spend years in committed effort and service to a company.

Relationship Styles strongly influence the categories of jobs one may be interested in, but that is only one of the essential variables in final career selection. Relationship aspects of work are generally less intimate and demanding than those of marriage and living together. Socially isolated individuals can spend successful careers in teaching, social work, and other socially related fields. In this way their need for human contact is met but they do not have to have children and deal with living with another individual.

Understanding Relationship Styles and individual character traits is important in assisting young people in developing a career plan. There are a large range of vocational possibilities in each category. Directors need to experience a sense of being empowered and make poor subordinates. Accommodators are well suited for occupations emphasizing interaction with people and service. They may prove to be good administrators and leaders. In general, Isolators tend not to make good supervisors or managers. Utilizing and accepting your Relationship Style as an important factor in making your vocational choices will help increase the likelihood of matching your unique interests with a successful place in the working world.

The Accommodator in the Working World

Accommodators possess characteristics that are highly desirable in many organizations. Accommodators, in general, are able to work well in corporate situations because their primary need is to be accepted and to fit in. Accommodators also do well in conventional careers such as in sales, banking and real estate, and in social careers in education, social service, and hospital settings.

Careers probably least viable for Accommodators are highly technical work or working with things rather than people: engineering, medical research, computer-based work, or assembly production work. Matching an Accommodator with a proper vocation involves developing an understanding of the person's unique characteristics and interests with an understanding of the educational requirements necessary to achieve career satisfaction. Accommodators may find law, teaching, or community service to be the best expression of their occupational potential. Accommodators with a high secondary trait of Director are well suited for political careers or public service, as are Directors with a high secondary trait of accommodation.

In many ways, accommodation is the easiest Relationship Style to assist vocationally. With more and more jobs becoming service-based rather than product-based, increasingly larger components of our labor force are involved in providing services to the public.

Guidelines for Accommodators

Accommodators, remember that you enjoy relating and being with people. This is your way of feeling connected and involved. Occupations that maximize the social nature of work are probably best suited for you: (1) Select the health professions, teaching, social work, or counseling, if you are willing to commit yourself to at least four years of higher education. (2) If you prefer more conventional work, think in terms of secretarial, sales, banking, or community-based occupations. (3) Avoid highly technical jobs or tasks that emphasize a product and its production rather than people. (4) Remember, Accommodators need a supportive employer. If you have a critical, controlling boss, your need for appreciation will be damaged. Do not accept this type of environment. Seek an employer who cares. This may be more important for you than the job itself. For example, Accommodators' key to success is working as a team player. Accommodators have superior capacity to adjust to corporate organizational structures. To maximize these assets, it is important to find an organization that values team players and rewards diligence. In this environment an Accommodator will flourish. Accommodators should avoid jobs that involve social isolation, or where the environment is competitive, hostile, and not supportive.

The Isolator in the Working World

Isolators show less predictable patterns of employment and vocational satisfaction. If they are socially compliant and withdrawing, Isolators can be enormously dedicated and committed employees in jobs that require minimal or controlled social contact. Isolators are also comfortable in jobs where work is oriented toward completing tasks rather than interacting with others. Examples would be assembly-line work, mechanical work, construction, and other product-oriented endeavors. Less disciplined and socially inadequate Isolators demonstrate severe underachievement and occupational instability. The career stability of Isolators involves multiple factors of self-esteem, acceptance of authority, and ability to comply with general social norms. Many Isolators who are competent and capable establish independent businesses, which may be accomplished in relative isolation from group settings.

Essentially, Isolators have three basic vocational styles. The first group includes compliant, nonassertive team members who seek stability and order. They are drawn to occupations in civil service, accounting, scientific and technical work, and product-oriented industries. They do well in environments where independent investigation is critical. The second group is independent Isolators whose primary businesses are usually product-oriented, with few or no employees. Finally, the third type of Isolator in the working world is the career-unstable Isolator, who tends to be underemployed or unemployed. Finding a comfortable working niche indicates an ability to adjust to structural and social norms. Many Isolators do not possess these characteristics. Isolators that don't may find that this inability to establish intimate relationships in their personal lives may directly translate into difficulty adjusting to other forms of relationships as well.

Some Thoughts on Isolators in the Working World

Isolators vary enormously in their adjustment to the working world. Disciplined and conservative Isolators make committed members of work teams. Isolators can be very responsive in social settings if intimate relationships are not emphasized. Many Isolators form small businesses where they can work on their own, and don't feel imposed upon by others. Unfortunately, Isolators who lack discipline and emotional stability make poor employees, and show histories of work instability. On the other hand, Isolators who enjoy technical work such as accounting, computer technology, and engineering prove to be extremely valuable members of corporate industrial systems. Isolators tend to work well in jobs that have reduced contact with the public, and that emphasize production and manufacturing.

Isolators can and do succeed in the working world. The difficulties they have in establishing long-term, intimate relationships may not have any significant impact on their work success; in fact, Isolators frequently substitute work and ambition for family life and activity. Isolators tend to do well in occupations that are not particularly demanding in terms of leadership skills. They are well suited for consistent jobs, to which they may dedicate themselves for a lifetime. Isolators are frequently excellent employees who value their job above all else. They are particularly well suited for product-oriented versus people-oriented work, where they feel a sense of mastery and control.

The Director in the Working World

Directors crave leadership roles, highly esteemed positions that involve demonstrating their skills and advanced education. Directors who have modified their insecurities with strong affiliation tendencies are the core population of our leaders, not only politically, but in industry and education. Independence of thought and freedom to control their work lives are essential to Directors. Many Directors are drawn to private enterprise or independent medical practice, because such jobs offer more autonomy. Directors do poorly in jobs where they are required to follow the instructions of supervisors and be passive team players. These professions are far better left to Accommodators, who are more affiliating. Directors want to lead, not be led. They are also drawn to professions where they can work independently.

An example of this may be a person who, as a child, fantasized becoming a lawyer, but eventually decided to forsake the law for a career in psychology, with an underlying desire to have a private practice. This is a Director with a fairly high level of affiliation. The selection of a career as a psychologist came from a mixture of an interest in people and a willingness to complete many years of higher education. Fierce desire for independence drew the person into private practice rather than community service-based psychology. Directors frequently have strong, definite career directions, and if their choices match their ability, they can be remarkably successful and enjoy enormous career satisfaction.

Some Thoughts for Directors

Directors come in all shapes and sizes. Some need the independence of self-employment. If you feel constricted in organizations and tend to be critical of restrictions and artificially imposed systems, work for yourself. Directors can motivate themselves and handle the unstructured nature of a free market economy. They can create new companies and run them skillfully. **Remember that in business, as in life, complete control is ultimately an illusion.** At best, we have limited control over the world we work in. Learning to cooperate and be less critical of co-workers and peers is important for most Directors. Directors need to examine their love of perfectionism and not try to impose it on others. Directors unable to do that are called tyrants, and unfortunately, many of you tyrant Directors seek positions of power in business and public administration. In summary, (1) Directors are well suited for leadership positions if they temper their critical side. (2) They are go-getters and can establish new companies, businesses, and professional practices. (3) Directors need more mobility and decision-making opportunities than the other two relationship types. They become frustrated, and will quit jobs that do not provide a challenging environment. (4) Directors who are not emotionally balanced make the worst employers. If you work for one, consider other options.

Directors need challenges, autonomy, and leadership roles. Directors can set up projects, run them efficiently, and challenge themselves to start new ones. They can function in corporate situations if they have independent management positions. They do not respond well to being subordinates, and are poorly suited to positions that demand this type of reduction in their need for self-expression. Directors are well suited for professional work, self-employment, and new ventures. Fortunately, our society rewards this type of independence of action and thought, and Directors are uniquely gifted in meeting these challenges.

Enlightened Leader or Tyrannical Dictator?

How often have you heard somebody say: "My boss is like a dictator?" As we have pointed out, Directors enjoy leadership positions, and some lack the empathy to handle people well. The reality of working for someone else is that you lose a certain degree of autonomy, and in order to succeed, you must conform to the desires of your supervisor or boss. Yet working with a controlling and critical boss is one of the more trying situations an employee faces. It is like reliving your childhood, except your parents at least loved you.

A negative, controlling, tyrannical dictator-type Director can demoralize an entire company and as history shows us, even a country. In order to survive in the workplace with negative Directors, employees frequently give up their dedication and desire, and go through the motions in a form of **professional depression.** It can be said that the working environment is more important than the job itself. Fortunately, not all Directors are tyrants. There are just as many who handle the power of being a boss very well and have genuine concern for their employees' needs.

We believe in and promote an enlightened leadership model. The primary difference between a leader and a tyrant is (1) recognition and concern about the feelings of others, as well as (2) the ability to evaluate the manner in which the leader communicates to others. When a leader acts kindly and is willing to apologize and request feedback from his subordinates, he or she has reached a level of enlightened leadership. **Clinical research has found that a company that is psychologically healthy is more economically effective.** For years companies have provided sensitivity training and classes in communication skills for executives in an attempt to improve their leadership skills. Learning to direct without being critical, to instruct without being demeaning and to make requests rather than demands involves awareness. Directors can be communicators and show empathy and genuine interest in the welfare of their employees; however, they must possess self-awareness and the desire to modify their controlling style.

The Relationship Assessment Scale and the Working World

We endorse the use of the Relationship Assessment Scale as a tool for vocational guidance and assessment. Within each Relationship Style there are enormous and varied possibilities. Remember, the core issue measured by the Relationship Scale is intimate relationship interaction. This only partially correlates to success in the working world. However, there are some basic principles that may be helpful in choosing your work, based on our measurement device. Your Relationship Style may prove to be a helpful concept as a marker for vocational counseling. Understanding your Relationship Style provides a piece of the puzzle in adjusting to the working world. Combined with appropriate vocational tests of interest and ability, your Relationship Style helps create a clear picture of your tendencies and character. A brief screening with the Relationship Assessment Scale can be worthwhile in developing the vocational profile of a new job applicant and assisting him or her in finding an appropriate niche in the workplace.

As outlined, Relationship Styles have an enormous impact on how well we adjust in the working world. In order to meet the demands of an ever-changing work environment, we must maximize our personal abilities. Each Relationship Style has characteristics that can be utilized to bring us personal success in our chosen career.

CHAPTER 12

INDIVIDUAL STYLE: PUTTING IT ALL TOGETHER

The central point of this book is to help you determine and understand your own unique Relationship Style. Whether you describe yourself as an Isolator, a Director, or an Accommodator, remember that these categories are essentially <u>neutral</u>. No style is superior; however, your style will have significant consequences in terms of your life. This book has attempted to demonstrate how your Relationship Style affects your actions, relationships and career choices. It shows you how you to modify your behavior, if you feel your style is undesirable in some areas and worthy of change.

We all need to feel empowered and proactive in living creatively. Yet we need to realize that our lives are shaped by our behavior. The manner in which you structure and live your life is important to its success in all areas. You are creating your life by making choices even if you barely acknowledge them. These choices are to a great extent the result of your Relationship Style. By now you have a basic understanding of your particular Relationship Style and that of others.

The next challenge is to apply this knowledge directly to your life and your current relationships. For example, after a failed relationship people often blame themselves or others for the failure. But relationships, like all human experiences, can end for many reasons. Assigning blame only creates the illusion that we can control the behavior of others. Ultimately most of our behaviors are understandable and fall into patterns throughout the course of our lives. Try to approach change without assigning blame.

Choosing to Be Single - A Valid Choice

In our contemporary culture there are many individuals, of all ages, who are still in pursuit of "Mr. or Ms. Right." A recent conversation with a 43-year-old man, a talented, attractive, and successful professional, illustrates this. In spite of years of dating he has steadfastly refused to marry and commit himself to anyone. We have discussed this many times and occasionally he still brings up the issue of meeting "Ms. Right." This is a deception Isolators use to avoid seeing how intent they are on maintaining their separateness and their sense of control in their lives. But the important issue is that there is absolutely nothing wrong with being single. Marriage is not a morally superior life choice. It is but a different one, with challenges and demands divergent from those of the single life.

We can apply this principle of understanding without judgment to any life choice. Many Directors refuse to acknowledge how their behavior can turn people off. This is most true when they attempt to dominate and control others in an authoritarian manner. Healthy Directors learn to temper their behavior and utilize their strength of character in a productive manner.

Accommodation is not Co-Dependency

Similarly, Accommodators have been condemned by pop psychology as co-dependent weaklings in need of assertiveness training. But, in reality, this is a distortion of what accommodation implies. Hopefully we have clarified that there are both healthy and unhealthy elements to accommodating others. Primarily, accommodating is a sensible position based on the realization that successful living requires mutual cooperation and flexibility.

The sales of self-help literature and relationship improvement programs have grown over the years because of tremendous public interest. People are searching for answers to the challenges of modern human relationships. Numerous self-proclaimed relationship experts promise much in their books and on television. They say that they can end your loneliness or fix your relationships with a few simple techniques. While we can appreciate their message, the truth of the matter is that there are really no simple solutions that address every individual situation for every person. We offer you no singular, simple solution to the complex issues surrounding human relationships. As psychotherapists we are amazed by promoters who imply that the answers to all human intimacy problems can be achieved by purchasing this set of tapes or that particular book. Many years of research indicate that psychotherapy can help individuals change, over time, when provided by competent professionals. However, this process is not a quick-fix approach.

Your Relationship Style, which developed during your childhood, will evolve throughout the course of your lifetime. When you begin to see yourself as you are to others, as well as recognizing your own internal struggles, you can remove emotional blinders, allowing meaningful change to occur. **Through this kind of important self-exploration process you can learn to accept who you are and learn to love your unique character. Remember, it is an ongoing process.**

Our goal in this book has been to provide a new direction for understanding one of the most confounding human experiences, that of relationships. This new direction is based on sound theoretical principles and years of practice and experience working with clients. We feel confident that the information and perspectives that we have provided will add to the collection of self-improvement tools available to you. With the information in this book you will be able to improve the quality of your life and your relationships.

REFERENCES

Alfred Adler, *Practice and Theory of Individual Psychology* (Patterson, N.J.: Littlefield, Adams, 1963).

Eric Berne, *Games People Play* (New York: Grove Press, 1964).

Erik Erikson, *Childhood and Society* (New York: Norton, 1950).

Karen Horney, *Our Inner Conflicts* (New York: Norton, 1945).

Arthur Janov, *The Primal Scream* (New York: Dell, 1970).

Alexander Lowen, *The Betrayal of the Body* (New York: Macmillan, 1967).

Robert Nideffer and Roger Sharpe, *A.C.T. Attention Control Training: How to Get Control of Your Mind Through Total Concentration* (New York: Wyden Books, 1978).

Frederick Perls, *Gestalt Therapy Verbatim* (New York: Bantam Books, 1969).

ABOUT THE AUTHORS

Kenneth Garett, Ph.D.

Dr. Kenneth Garett is a licensed psychologist who resides in Palm Springs, California, with his wife Tamara and their daughter Renee and son Alexander. Dr. Garett, an expert in child development and family dynamics, has appeared on many national television shows. He has taught psychology at California State University and Pepperdine University. He maintains an active practice in family treatment, as well as providing advanced training to mental health professionals throughout Southern California. Dr. Garett has lived in Latin America and is considered an expert in pre-Columbian art and ethnic art. He has practiced yoga for over 25 years and studied in India. He enjoys hiking, swimming and spending time with his family.

William Rose, Ph.D.

Dr. William Rose is a psychotherapist who resides and practices in Southern California. He has worked with children, adolescents and adults in both inpatient and outpatient settings. His area of specialization includes individual, couples, family and group psychotherapy. He also consults, provides psychological evaluations and enjoys exploring the clinical use of hypnosis. Dr. Rose's personal interests include nature, fitness, photography, sculpting, and writing.

For more information about this book and other publications by:

Williams Publishing
Books that Inform, Educate and Inspire

We welcome your responses and suggestions. If you would like to share your thoughts or feelings after reading this book, please write or call and tell us about your experience. We especially would like to hear about any positive changes or rewarding expeiences in your life related to this book.

Other fine books available:
* *Relationship Styles & Patterns Workbook*
(ISBN: 0-9666906-4-8)
* *Relationship Styles & Patterns: Audio Book on cassette*
(ISBN: 0-9666906-8-0)

To order:
Call toll-free (800) 444-2524
Credit cards accepted

To contact the authors regarding their schedules for up-coming workshops and seminars or to be on our mailing list for our other outstanding publications please contact:

Williams Publishing
4766 Park Granada Suite #209
Calabasas, California 91302
Telephone: (818) 591-0576
Toll Free: (877) WP-BOOKS
Fax: (818) 591-1682 E-mail: PSBill@aol.com
To contact Dr. Garett call toll-free: (800) 335-9859
To contact Dr. Rose call toll-free: (877) 972-6657